50 Great Adventures

Front cover, top to bottom: Sofia Brignone; Courtesy of Guinness Storehouse Museum; MILD Graphics; John Gollings, © RPBW, Renzo Piano Building Workshop; © John Warburton-Lee/John Warburton-Lee Photography

Prestel Verlag
Königinstrasse 9, D-80539 Munich
Tel. +49 (89) 38 17 09-0
Fax +49 (89) 38 17 09-35
www.prestel.de

Prestel Publishing Ltd.
4, Bloomsbury Place, London WC1A 2QA
Tel. +44 (020) 7323-5004
Fax +44 (020) 7636-8004

Prestel Publishing
900 Broadway, Suite 603,
New York, N.Y. 10003
Tel. +1 (212) 995-2720
Fax +1 (212) 995-2733
www.prestel.com

Library of Congress Control Number:
2005904403

The Deutsche Bibliothek holds a record of this publication in the Deutsche Nationalbibliographie; detailed bibliographical data can be found under: http://dnb.dde.de

Prestel books are available worldwide. Please contact your nearest bookseller or one of the above addresses for information concerning your local distributor.

Editorial direction: Philippa Hurd
Design, layout and typesetting: SMITH, London
Origination: Icon, London
Printing and binding: Print Consult, Munich

Printed in Germany on acid-free paper

ISBN 3-7913-3434-9

50 Great Adventures

Extraordinary Places and the People who Built Them

Jonathan Lee

PRESTEL

MUNICH • BERLIN • LONDON • NEW YORK

LIVE

WORK

PRAY

PLAY

STAY

Within these pages you'll travel around the world to meet an eccentric English earl, a Ming emperor and a French postman, a Fascist and a communist, eco-warriors, utopian idealists, Indian maharanas, cowboys, the power-hungry, the erudite, the fabulously wealthy, and the borderline insane.

In my travels I've come across some truly extraordinary man-made places, from stunning mansions, subterranean auditoria, hotels and churches to bizarre houses and breathtaking sports grounds. I've been particularly interested in places that blur the boundary between people and nature. This book comprises a collection of such spectacular spaces. Many people will call this architectural or landmark tourism, but I prefer to see it as the tourism of ideas.

It's true that we often travel to rest and recharge, but we're increasingly looking for insights into different cultures, new ways of thinking and, more often than not, for adventure. These 50 stories are starting points for such adventures. How you get there is up to you. I've included advice that will send you on plane trips and bumpy bus rides, on treks across icy Nordic fjords and hundreds of metres beneath the surface of the earth. But if you choose to go no further than your armchair that's fine too. This is a guide for adventures of the mind as much as the body.

I've tried to get under the skin of these 50 places by focusing on the people that made them happen and the ideas that inspired them. When I visited many of them I asked four key questions: who built them, what were they trying to achieve, how on earth did they do it and, above all, how did they get the idea in the first place? Sometimes I found the answer in a well-written guidebook or in a glossy pamphlet I was given at the door. But the best answers came from the people involved. Why? Because people tell good stories and their enthusiasm captures the drama and atmosphere of a place best. I've tried to make this storytelling an important element of this book.

At the heart of this endeavour is a group of people who have had the courage to create the extraordinary, the ground-breaking, or the just plain barmy. Each person is different, but they all share two qualities: a good idea and the energy to drive it through. Jobs and pension schemes, mortgages and health-care plans, the chance of promotion—there are more reasons than ever not to take a risk in life, not to change things or break the rules. But these people did, and most made a huge success of it. I've been inspired by many of these achievements, and I hope that you will be too. If this book prompts you to ask "why can't I do something like that?", and perhaps even start planning such a project, then it really will have succeeded.

In many cases, I've added to my personal experience of the place by talking to these people direct. And when this hasn't been possible, I've tried to speak to the best available experts in the field. My interviewees are based all around the world from Australia's Graeme Kelleher, creator of the world's largest living reef aquarium, to Bernard Khoury, the architect of a monument-cum-restaurant in former war-torn Beirut, and Yngve Bergqvist, the founder of Lapland's Ice Hotel, which melts away into the river only to be built anew every year.

I've grouped the contents into five themes—live, work, pray, play, and stay—partly because we spend our lives engaged in these activities, but also because I think these five ideas are drivers for the act of creativity itself. Artists often look to these pursuits to create their work; designers and architects are no different, and their output is usually a tangible, long-lasting product—an idea rendered real in a structure that you can visit, touch, and explore. It's this aspect that interested me most: built structures aren't just about functional concrete and stone and glass—they're creativity made manifest.

These projects show how interconnected some of the world's big thinkers and ideas are. For example, Louis I. Kahn taught Mario Botta, Paolo Soleri was a student of Frank Lloyd Wright, and Javier Senosiain was inspired by Antoni Gaudí. Evidence of such influential relationships abounds within these pages, but there's a more subtle kinship going on too: individuals have reached similar conclusions, even though they have been working independently on different sides of the globe. Highway inspector Nek Chand created his Rock Garden in India, but postman Ferdinand Cheval spent 30 years building another example of Outsider Art thousands of miles away in France. In the 1960s, the UK-based Archigram Group was experimenting with "plug-in" cities and buildings that evolved according to users' needs, while in Japan Kisho Kurokawa built an apartment tower block that did exactly that.

I have focussed on relatively modern examples for one key reason: many of these structures are tackling issues that affect us all today—the most pressing one being how the human race can survive without destroying the natural environment more than it has already. For example, how can we treat the earth with more respect while still reaping the benefits of mass tourism? Take a look at Tim Smit's Eden Project in England, home to the world's largest conservatory, or César Manrique's eco-inspired houses and underground performance spaces in the Canary Islands. How can we persuade squabbling religious factions and the secular community to talk to each? Norbert Cymbalista's Synagogue and Jewish Heritage Center in Israel offers a possible solution. How can we preserve the threatened culture of indigenous peoples? New Caledonia's Tjibaou Cultural Centre and Norway's Sámi Parliament Building offer ideas. And how can we build stronger communities and cut crime and pollution? Arcosanti, Paolo Soleri's experimental town in the Arizona desert, is attempting to achieve just this. These people don't pretend to have found all the answers, and some projects may have failed outright, but the process of exploration has proved invaluable. Most importantly, these people are actually doing something rather than dream, procrastinate, or give up.

This book isn't limited to exploring big-budget, global ideas. It contains everyday inspiration for people like you and me too, whether that be building a new extension on your house, thinking up a new business idea, improving the quality of your neighbourhood, or, of course, planning your next holiday. For me, this book goes to the heart of why we travel: to discover people and ideas that can change the way we think. I hope this book takes you somewhere new.

Accordion House
Sweden

Wander deep into Sweden's Glaskogen nature reserve and strike out towards the banks of Lake Övre Gla. If you're lucky you'll spot a giant slug-like creature, quietly grazing among the forest's weatherworn boulders.

"The most important goal we wanted to achieve was that the building would blend in with its surroundings without having to be invisible. So on top of the granite rocks we built a sculpture that, in time, would become like a rock itself." Boris Zeisser, architect.

Far left: the Dragspelhuset in its forest setting.
Left: a view across Lake Övre Gla in the Glaskogen nature reserve.

What you've actually found is the Dragspelhuset or "accordion house"—an extraordinary summer residence that expands and contracts with the seasons. During the winter the Dragspelhuset forms a neat cocoon, sporting a double skin to keep out the cold. But in the summer it morphs and extends to form an idyllic forest hideaway, reclining among silver birches.

The house represents a canny circumvention of planning regulations. Maartje Lammers and Boris Zeisser found an 18th-century fisherman's cabin in the heart of Glaskogen—a 28,000-hectare national park with stunning lakes and forests that's alive with elk, fox, roe, badger and the odd wolf. The husband-and-wife partnership at the helm of Rotterdam-based 24H Architecture set about planning the cabin's renovation, but soon came up against local bylaws, which prevented them extending the house by more than 30 square metres.

Their solution was ingenious. They built a core static bedroom, kitchen and dining space, and then designed a 4.5-metre cantilevered lounge section to extend over a nearby waterfall. Imagine a giant matchbox, with the box adding another 15 square metres of living space. The result is the perfect summer retreat for the couple and their young daughter, and as the temporary extension has no foundations, it keeps the planning inspectors happy.

A night or two in the Dragspelhuset is a pure Hans Christian Anderson fantasy. Reindeer skins line the snug interior and there's even a wood-fuelled stove, happily puffing out smoke through the creature's snout. The place is eco-friendly too, with power provided by solar panels. The whole structure blends into the rocky forest landscape thanks to a zero-maintenance cedar-shingle exterior, which greys and softens with age. For once, we doff our collective cap to unbending planners.

HOW TO GET THERE

The nearest international airports are Oslo (250 km) and Göteborg (250 km), and there's a smaller airport at Karlstad (100 km). Take a train or bus to Arvika, pick up the bus 162 to Glava and hike the bracing 16 km to Lenungshammar, which is a good starting point for walks throughout the park, and hosts cabins, a camping site, and information centre. From here you can hike to Barlingshult where you'll find the Dragspelhuset.

Glaskogens Naturreservat
SE-671 81 Arvika
Sweden
Tel: +46 (0)570 440 70
Email: glaskogen@arvika.se
www.glaskogen.se
www.dragspelhuset.com

Below: the warm confines of the Dragspulhuset, complete with reindeer skins.
Right: the Dragspelhuset's cantilivered lounge extends over a waterfall.

The Royal Pavilion
England

This pavilion started life as a simple seaside farmhouse—until an extravagant British prince looked east for inspiration.

"The most extraordinary compound of talent, wit, buffoonery, obstinacy and good feelings, in short, a medley of the most opposite qualities, with a great preponderance of good—that I ever saw in any character in my life." The Duke of Wellington on George IV.

Left: George IV (1762–1830) The Prince was a keen music fan; his Music Room (far left) was lit by nine lotus-shaped chandeliers. Right: the full grandeur of Brighton Pavilion.

HOW TO GET THERE
The nearest airport is Gatwick, 30 minutes away by road or rail. Brighton is 90 km from London and it takes less than an hour to travel from the capital by train. There are also regular buses from London Bridge and London Victoria station. You'll find the Royal Pavilion in Brighton town centre, a 15-minute walk from the train station.

The Royal Pavilion
Brighton BN1 1EE
England
Tel: +44 (0) 1273 290900
Email: visitor.services@brighton-hove.gov.uk
www.royalpavilion.org.uk

In 1785 the dissolute son of George III married the divorced Catholic Maria Fitzherbert. The wedding—illegal under a recent Royal Marriages Act—was held in secret, and the Prince of Wales proceeded to rent a farmhouse in Brighton to be near his new bride.

After 20 years of heavy drinking, gambling, womanising and, perhaps worst of all, adding frivolous oriental and neo-classical elements to the farmhouse, the whimsical Prince asked architect John Nash to transform the entire building into an Indian-style pavilion. The result is an extraordinary mixture of oriental and Mogul styles: a quirky high-point of Regency architecture or an ostentatious dog's breakfast, depending on your view.

Whatever your tastes, be prepared for a visual assault of headache-inducing proportions when you visit. Under the onion-shaped domes and minarets you'll find a place awash with gold leaf, dolphin motifs, Oriental columns, carved palm trees, dragon chimneypieces, and gilded serpents.

The tour starts in the Octagon Hall, with its vast ceiling designed in the shape of an Asiatic tent. Head through the central 54-metre Chinese-style Long Gallery and you reach the banqueting room's extraordinary centrepiece: a huge carved dragon perching on a 10-metre-high crystal chandelier. Also, don't miss the Music Room with its lotus-shaped gasoliers, murals, and a scallop-shell dome.

John Nash's friendship with the Prince did the architect's bank balance a great deal of good: his other royal commissions included London's Buckingham Palace and Regent's Park terraces. But things weren't quite so rosy for the Prince. Ascending to the throne upon the death of his insane father in 1820, George IV spent his 10-year reign in a haze of laudanum and alcohol-induced self-delusion. He died a national joke. His daughter, Queen Victoria, gave the Royal Pavilion to Brighton in 1850.

"The Pavilion is a strange, odd, Chinese looking place, both outside and inside. Most of the rooms are low and I can only see a morsel of the sea from one of my sitting room windows." Queen Victoria.

Left, clockwise from top left: your tour will take you through the Long Gallery (used for playing cards, music, and conversation); the Yellow Bow Rooms (the bedrooms of George IV's brothers); the South Galleries, which were used by the Prince's residential guests; and The Saloon.

Arcosanti
USA

Utopia may take many forms, but few of them look as weird as Arcosanti—a mélange of sliced domes and quirky geometry amid the arid Arizona desert.

The Vaults (opposite, top) host performances and events.
Bottom left: the ubiquitous wind bells, which help fund the project.
Right: an aerial view of the city.

"The problem I am confronting is the present design of cities only a few stories high, stretching outward in unwieldy sprawl for miles. As a result of their sprawl, they literally transform the earth, turn farms into parking lots and waste enormous amounts of time and energy transporting people, goods and services over their expanses. My solution is urban implosion rather than explosion."
Paolo Soleri (1919–).

HOW TO GET THERE
The best airport is Phoenix Sky Harbor. You'll find Arcosanti in central Arizona, 100 km north of Phoenix. It's just off the Interstate Highway 17, and you need to take the Cordes Junction turn-off, exit 262. The final 4 km are pretty bumpy, so it helps if you're driving a decent SUV. Arcosanti hosts numerous arts festivals including classical music and jazz concerts, so check the website before you visit. It's possible to stay overnight as long as you book in advance.

Arcosanti
HC 74, Box 4136
Mayer, AZ 86333 USA
Tel: +1 (928) 632 7135
Email: info@arcosanti.org
www.arcosanti.org

Founded in 1970, Arcosanti is an evolving "urban laboratory" designed to prove that towns can be both functional and eco-friendly. Drive a dusty hour or so north of Phoenix and you'll find students, interns, and volunteers beavering away, developing a metropolis of multi-use buildings, low-impact dorm housing, recycling centres, and greenhouses. The gentle tinkling of ceramic and bronze wind bells accompanies your wander round, a constant reminder of the town's bizarre source of funding and origins.

In the late 1940s Italian architect Paolo Soleri had just finished a stint in Arizona under the tutelage of Frank Lloyd Wright, perhaps the US's greatest architect. The apprenticeship inspired Soleri's theories of living architectural forms and progressive urban planning.
In 1950 Soleri returned to Italy and was commissioned to design a ceramics factory. This was a pivotal project, as through it Soleri acquired a sophisticated grasp of silt-casting and ceramic processes, going on to design his award-winning wind bell, the mammoth sales of which bankrolled his Arcosanti project. The town now produces wind bells in industrial quantities, with sales helping fund the experiment to this day.

Arcosanti is a living exploration of Soleri's theory of Arcology, a fusion of architecture and ecology. The aim is to create the very antithesis of the big, bad sprawling metropolis: a car-free, small footprint settlement of compact housing and shared public space. The project makes full use of sustainable energy and recycling, thus avoiding many of the social problems that sully contemporary urban life.

If this all sounds a bit idealistic, it is. Arcosanti is still an urban prototype that's more about theory than practice. Originally designed to house around 5,000 people, Arcosanti's permanent population barely exceeds 100 and the pace of construction is painfully slow. However, the town's educational record is admirable: more than 6,000 people have attended workshops (which Soleri himself still goes to) and more than a million day-trippers have visited. After all, where else can you pick up a beautifully crafted wind bell and a glimpse of utopia in a day?

Castle Drogo
England

A 33-year-old millionaire, a Norman baron and the British Empire's finest architect—the story of Castle Drogo is the stuff of far-fetched Hollywood epics. Except in this case, the tale happens to be true.

Far left: one of Castle Drogo's impressive granite hallways, this one featuring a portrait of Julius Drewe.

Left: Julius Drewe (1856–1931).
Right: Castle Drogo sits high above the Teign gorge on the edge of Dartmoor.

Julius Drewe was a successful tea merchant who founded the English grocery chain, Home and Colonial Stores. Having made his millions, he retired in 1889 at just 33 years old. Then, while researching his family history, he became convinced that he was a descendent of Drogo de Teigne, a 12th-century Norman baron who gave his name to the small village of Drewsteignton, on Dartmoor, in Devon. The discovery was particularly useful for someone of self-made rather than inherited wealth.

The grocery magnate decided to build a home on his new-found ancestor's estate, choosing a dramatic spot nearly 300 metres above the Teign gorge. But rejecting the standard stately home *du jour*, he drew inspiration from his supposed baronial blood and commissioned a mock medieval castle. Sparing no expense, his architect of choice was Sir Edwin Lutyens, the man responsible for swathes of New Delhi, London's cenotaph and numerous stately homes. Drewe lay the foundation stone on April 4, 1911—his 55th birthday. But building his labour of love wasn't glitch-free: initial designs had to be scaled down amid fears that the place would be too large to inhabit, and labour shortages thwarted grander elements such a four-storey gate-tower. The ancestral seat was completed in 1930—just a year before Drewe died.

Although the castle's exterior exudes medieval austerity, you'll be pleasantly surprised upon crossing the threshold—under a portcullis, of course. Vaulted ceilings and Flemish tapestry-adorned walls lend warmth and character, while vast mullioned windows provide inspiring views down the valley and across the moor. A highlight is the Edwardian elegance of the bathrooms and dressing rooms, while the kitchens and servants' quarters provide a fascinating snapshot of life below stairs. Don't miss the grounds and gardens, which feature a series of terraces leading up to a huge circular croquet lawn bordered by an immaculate yew hedge.

The "last castle to be built in England" has now become an ongoing labour of love for a new clan—the family donated it to leading heritage charity the National Trust in 1974.

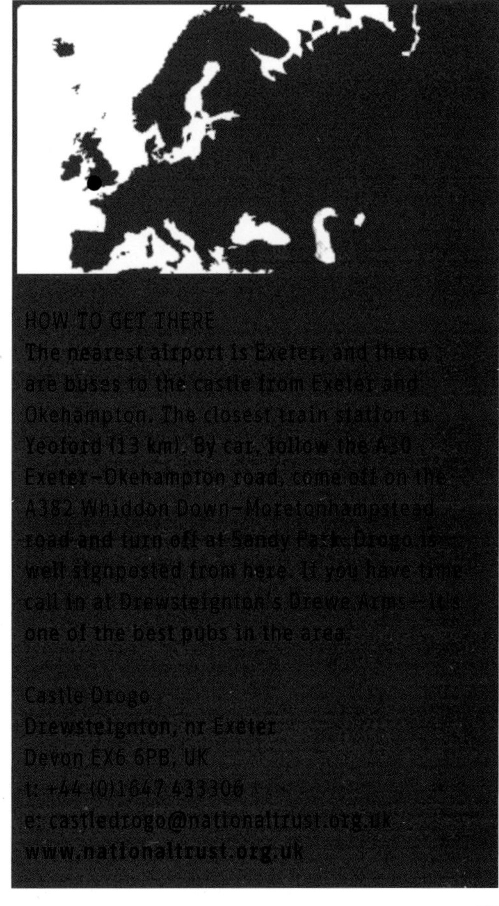

HOW TO GET THERE
The nearest airport is Exeter, and there are buses to the castle from Exeter and Okehampton. The closest train station is Yeoford (13 km). By car, follow the A30 Exeter–Okehampton road, come off on the A382 Whiddon Down–Moretonhampstead road and turn off at Sandy Park. Drogo is well signposted from here. If you have time call in at Drewsteignton's Drewe Arms—it's one of the best pubs in the area.

Castle Drogo
Drewsteignton, nr Exeter
Devon EX6 6PB, UK
t: +44 (0)1647 433306
e: castledrogo@nationaltrust.org.uk
www.nationaltrust.org.uk

Below, clockwise from top left: the library (where Lutyens even designed the bookshelves), the bathroom, dining room, and vaulted ceiling. Right: the kitchen with its huge circular table centrepiece.

Nakagin Capsule Tower
Japan

Moving house ranks as one of life's biggest stresses. But in Tokyo there are residents who might never have to pack up their possessions ever again.

"The 21st century will be one in which fusion, fission, steam, and water-generated electrical plants will exist in symbiosis." Kisho Kurokawa (1934–).

Far left: the ever-changing tower.
Left: The busy streets of Tokyo's Ginza district.

Built in Tokyo in 1972, the Nakagin Capsule Tower is an apartment block that can be configured entirely to meet its occupants' needs. You're single? Just take one studio-space-sized room. A few years pass and you have a family? Simply bolt on a few interconnecting rooms to create more space. Capsules are assembled off-site and delivered complete with furniture, telephone points, and stereos, and are slotted into place using high-tension bolts. The building was designed with easy maintenance in mind: shorter lifespan elements such as mechanical parts and piping are separated from the main structure to make servicing and replacement as easy as possible.

The tower was designed by Japanese architect, Kisho Kurokawa, and is perhaps now regarded as more a symbol of architectural experimentalism than a practicable way to house the masses. Kurokawa was a founder member of the Metabolism movement, founded in the 1960s to wrestle with basic social problems such as overcrowding and waste. Inspired by the natural processes of metamorphosis and symbiosis, the Metabolists argued that buildings should be capable of organic growth, and should metamorphose to meet users' evolving needs. The Metabolists shared a great deal of ground with Britain's Archigram Group, famous for its "plug-in" cities. But while their ideological cousins' ideas were confined largely to the drawing board, the Nakagin Tower was actually built and became an icon of the movement.

Metabolism petered out in the early 1970s, but Kurokawa has continued to design structures, employing similar philosophies across Asia, Europe and his home country. Take a look at Japan's Nagoya City Art Museum, his extension to the Van Gogh Museum in Amsterdam, and the Japanese–German Center in Berlin. Kurokawa has also published numerous books on the subject, his *Philosophy of Symbiosis* being a good meaty introduction.

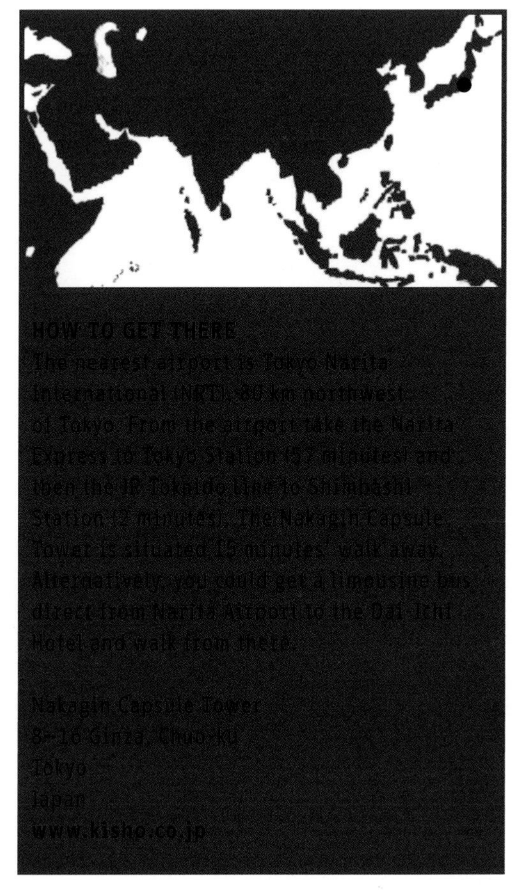

HOW TO GET THERE
The nearest airport is Tokyo Narita International (NRT), 80 km northwest of Tokyo. From the airport take the Narita Express to Tokyo Station (57 minutes) and then the JR Tokaido Line to Shimbashi Station (2 minutes). The Nakagin Capsule Tower is situated 15 minutes' walk away. Alternatively, you could get a limousine bus direct from Narita Airport to the Dai-Ichi Hotel and walk from there.

Nakagin Capsule Tower
8-16 Ginza, Chuo-ku
Tokyo
Japan
www.kisho.co.jp

"We must learn a lesson from the subtle behavior of living organisms and from software. In other words, the mating of the automation of man-made technology and the bio of living things will give birth to the technology of a new human society. I call this hybrid product biomation." Kisho Kurokawa.

Left: rooms are bolted into place as required. Below: a Nakagin interior—mod cons come as standard.

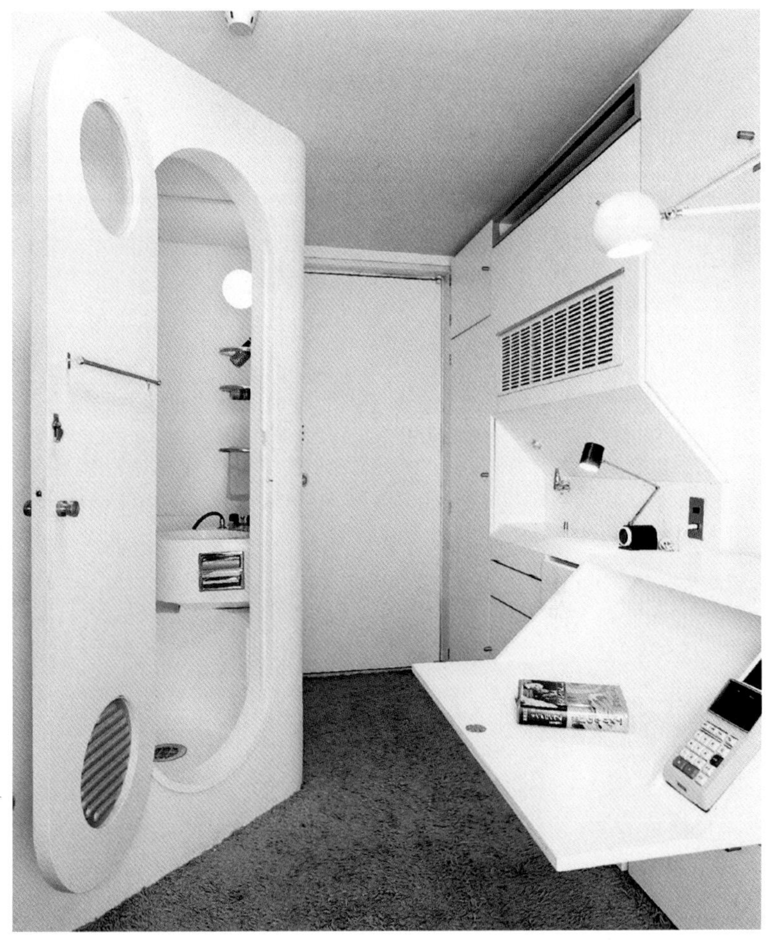

The Shark House
Mexico

Jonah may have disagreed, but for Javier Senosiain there are few better addresses than a mammoth aquatic creature.

The house started life as one-bedroomed dwelling, and was only christened "The Shark" by builders when its new studio, girls' bedroom, and terrace with a semi-covered jacazzi conspired to produce such a distinctive shape.

At first glance the Shark House looks like the product of an unhinged mind. Its snout, neat dorsal fin, and huge fusiform flank are an entertaining rendering of a shark's anatomy, but how practical can it really be? The answer, it turns out, is extremely practical. A tour deep into the creature's gullet reveals that the Mexican architect has designed every detail with precision and purpose. The snout houses his studio, providing inspirational views across Mexico City's Los Remedios national park. The semi-subterranean "body" features bedrooms, TV room, living room, kitchen, and even a jacuzzi.

The whole place has a retro-futuristic feel and is full of functional nooks and crannies that allow its occupants to go about their business in an atmosphere of relaxed "collective privacy". All walls curve seamlessly into ceilings and floors, emphasising the fluidity and harmony of the space. Sounds like the perfect family home? That's exactly what it's meant to be: Senosiain originally designed the place with only one bedroom, but as his family grew he extended it to accommodate his wife and their daughters.

The building is primarily made of ferro-cement, with most of the furniture fused to its structure. Senosiain firmly believes that physical contact with the floor engenders feelings of freedom.

The Shark House is one of the best examples of Senosiain's biomorphic aesthetic. Walking in the footsteps of organic architects such as Gaudí and Frank Lloyd Wright, the Mexican is a leading exponent of design inspired by nature—except that in this case he's replicated an organic shape in its entirety rather than re-fashioned just a part of it.

And there's one key thing that proves the Shark House is a practical home, rather than a madcap celebrity architect showcase: when you visit, Senosiain insists you take your shoes off at the door.

HOW TO GET THERE

The Shark House is situated in Vista del Valle at the edge of Los Remedios national park, a 400-hectare park situated around 24 km north of the centre of Mexico City. The best way to get there from the city centre is by taxi.

The Shark House
Vista del Valle
Mexico City, Mexico
www.bioarquitectura.com

Far left, top: Senosiain's studio looks through the jaws of the creature out across Los Remedios national park.
Far left, bottom and left: there is little moveable furniture and most elements are fused to the structure of the building throughout, including in bedrooms and reading nooks.

Butch and Sundance's Cabin
Argentina

Wander along the eastern bank of Patagonia's Blanco River and you'll find a log cabin quietly falling to bits next to the spine of the Andes.

"Like lots of cowboy outlaws in them days Butch and me liked to give lots of money to the poor, the needy, and the deserving. In this way we made sort of Robin Hoods of ourselves in our own eyes, gained a lot of popularity and protection from the public, and squared ourselves in our own estimation."
A member of Butch and Sundance's gang, the Wild Bunch.

Opposite, top: Aladín Sepúlveda, who was born and lived his whole life in the cabin, until relatively recently.

Right: five members of the Wild Bunch, pictured in 1900. Butch Cassidy (Robert Leroy Parker) and the Sundance Kid (Harry Longbaugh) are far right and far left respectively.

HOW TO GET THERE
The nearest airport is Esquel, although you'll probably be travelling around the country using Argentina's excellent bus network. Butch and Sundance's house lies 12 km north of Cholila along the RP71. It's not signposted, so if you're coming by bus you have to ask the driver to make a special stop. Once you've wandered around the house, make sure you carry on down the track to La Casa de Piedra, a Welsh teahouse with a beautiful garden and excellent cakes.

Butch and Sundance's Cabin
Near La Casa de Piedra
El Blanco, Cholila, Patagonia
Argentina
www.crimelibrary.com/gangsters_outlaws/outlaws/cassidy/1.html

If you'd knocked on the front door of this shack just over a century ago, you would have been welcomed in by Robert LeRoy Parker and Harry Longabaugh—otherwise known as Butch Cassidy and the Sundance Kid. And despite their gun-toting reputation you probably would have spent a couple of hours chewing over innocuous pursuits such as cattle-rearing, rather than daring bank heists or train robberies.

The story of the two outlaws has been romanticised beyond belief: the 1969 film perpetuated the myth of a pair of Robin Hoods of the Wild West. Refreshingly, their Argentinian sojourn is beyond doubt, and their cabin worm-eaten proof of an understandable attempt to embark on a quieter life.

The journey to the cabin started in 1900 when Butch and Sundance robbed the First National Bank in Nevada. With the Pinkerton National Detective Agency on their tail, the bandits fled south to Argentina, fired up by stories of Patagonian gauchos and Wild West-style prairies. They found the perfect spot in the verdant Cholila valley. Butch built a neat log cabin, and the outlaws settled down to a crime-free life with Sundance's girlfriend, Etta Place. Investing the spoils of their bank job in a 5,000-hectare ranch they successfully farmed cattle, sheep and horses. Neighbours reportedly found the trio extremely friendly.

A wander around the four rooms of the outlaws' cabin makes your spine tingle: you can almost hear Butch strumming samba rhythms on his guitar while Sundance and Etta whirl and turn on the mud floors. It was inhabited until relatively recently, and you can still see scraps of wallpaper peeling off the walls. And despite a design poorly suited to the harsh climate, the whole structure still stands defiantly against the fierce Patagonian winds.

The bandits' quiet life couldn't last. In 1905 they returned to their bad old ways, and held up a bank in nearby Santa Cruz. No one's sure quite why they left the ranch, although Etta's return to the US to have a baby may have prompted a change of heart, or local farmers may have tipped off the law, forcing them to sell up.

There are also numerous versions of the duo's demise, their 1908 mine payroll robbery being the most popular. After the theft Butch and Sundance supposedly took refuge in the Bolivian village of San Vicente, but found themselves hopelessly outnumbered by soldiers. They died in a massive shoot-out, their blazing "last stand" providing the ultimate Hollywood ending.

Forbidden City
China

The number nine signifies longevity in Chinese culture, so no wonder the world's biggest palace complex with its 9,999 rooms established an empire lasting five centuries.

Far left: the palace's moat and gate tower.
Left: an aerial view of the city, which covers 74 hectares.

Imagine the scene: you're a usurping Ming emperor with a cut-throat attitude and ambitious plans to expand your empire. Having eliminated your opponents in a grisly fashion, you need to stamp your authority over your ministers, subjects, and the vast territories that lie within your sights. For Emperor Yong Le the answer lay in moving the capital north from Nanjing to Beijing and creating a palace where ordinary citizens were unable to tread.

The third Ming ruler commissioned the palace in 1406, three years into his reign. It took a million workers 14 years to build the imperial seat, with every aspect designed to reinforce the dynasty's supremacy and score a political, cultural, or hierarchical point. It housed the emperor and his family plus eunuchs, concubines, and servants.

The complex covers 74 hectares protected by a 52-metre-wide moat and a 10-metre-high wall, and the style of windows, doors, and ceilings reflect the status of each building. Areas such as the Hall of Supreme Harmony, the Hall of Celestial Purity, east and west palaces, and four imposing entrances have secured its reputation as the finest example of traditional Chinese architecture.

By the time was palace was completed in 1420, Yong Le was well on the way to creating an empire to justify such palatial extravagance. Although his mercilessness alarmed his administration, he is now regarded as the most competent of Ming rulers. Known as "The Consolidator" he oversaw a series of maritime expeditions sailing as far as East Africa and the Indian Ocean. And with the incorporation of South and Southeast Asia into China's "tribute" system—securing strong trade links and far-reaching political influence—the empire flourished.

The Forbidden City became the home and power base of 24 emperors of the Ming and Qing dynasties, who ruled China from 1368 to 1911. The last emperor was routed from the complex in 1924 and it was awarded UNESCO World Cultural Heritage Site status in 1987.

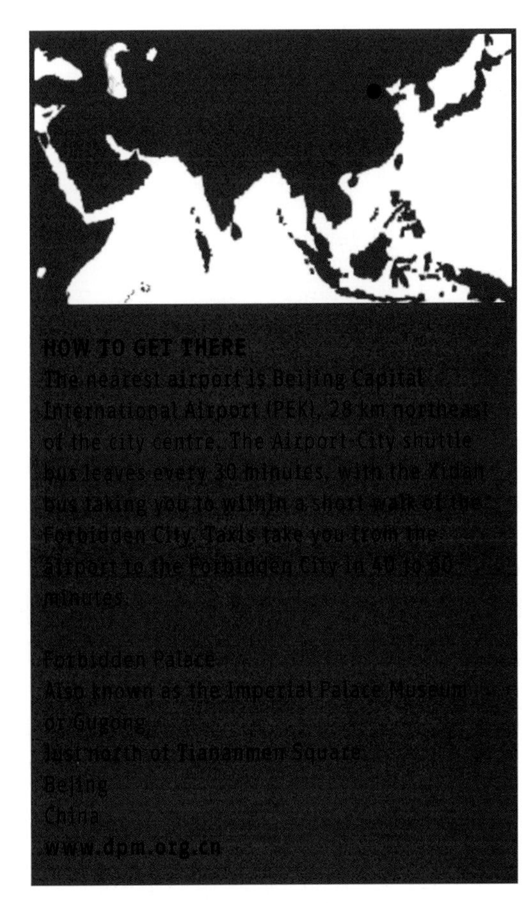

HOW TO GET THERE
The nearest airport is Beijing Capital International Airport (PEK), 28 km northeast of the city centre. The Airport-City shuttle bus leaves every 30 minutes, with the Xidan bus taking you to within a short walk of the Forbidden City. Taxis take you from the airport to the Forbidden City in 40 to 60 minutes.

Forbidden Palace
Also known as the Imperial Palace Museum or Gugong
Just north of Tiananmen Square
Beijing
China
www.dpm.org.cn

Highlights of the palace include the Meridian gate (left), the Halls of Harmony, which are situated on a tiered marble terrace (right), the throne in the Hall of Preserved Harmony, used by the Emperor for official ceremonies (bottom right) and the 52-metre-wide moat (bottom left).

Free Spirit Spheres
Canada

Around three million years ago man's ancestors left the trees for life on terra firma. But if Tom Chudleigh has his way, the forest canopy beckons once again.

Far left: visitors access the spheres using wooden walkways. Vancouver Island offers a wilderness of forests, lakes, and mountains (left).

What the sphere does do is force us into a cooperative living arrangement with the forest. The trees have to be nurtured and protected to keep the sphere safe. I think they create a little bubble of altered space in the midst of a confused world."
Tom Chudleigh (1951–).

If you're an adventurous type who's not too bothered about domestic mod cons—or living anywhere near the ground for that matter—then Tom Chudleigh's Free Spirit Spheres might be just the address you're after. You and three friends can sleep in one of the three-metre-wide durable globes, which gently rock 30 metres above the forest floor. And when you're tired of your patch of forest, simply unhitch and move to another leafy glade.

Being inside one of Tom's spheres is akin to a spell below decks in a lovingly crafted boat. You have the luxury of a double bed, sofa and galley area with counter and cupboards. The place is wired for power and telephone, and windows provide a bird's-eye view of the forest canopy. Plummeting night-time temperatures are kept at bay by a 750-watt electric heater.

For a glimpse of Tom's inspiration—and to test-drive the spheres for yourself—head for the tiny village of Errington, at the foot of Canada's Vancouver Island mountains. In the wilds of British Columbia you've a choice of hiking through the cedar forests, swimming in crystal-clear lakes, or just marvelling at spectacular waterfalls and gorges. The area is quite a magnet for artists and craftspeople, and it's no wonder Tom was inspired by the "head space" afforded by living close to nature. Keen to minimise our impact on the environment, Tom came up with a portable sphere that could be removed in just a day, disappearing without a trace. Tom's hand-crafted wooden spheres cost from around $100,000 each and he is now producing fully fitted fibreglass versions selling from $30,000. You can buy them in kit form for a lot less.

There's only one downside to sphere life—there's no bathroom so you have to shimmy down from your eyrie to perform your ablutions. But as you read this Tom is working on a washroom/shower/sauna hub complete with an effluent-processing system that will serve a colony of spheres via connected walkways.

Il Vittoriale
Italy

Garda is the largest and purest of the Italian lakes, boasting natural beauty on a breathtaking scale. On its western shore is the legacy of one of the most bizarre characters of modern times.

Below left: Il Vittoriale's Dalmation Square, with its central "pilum" and two grinding stones, a remnant of an old mill on the property. The base is decorated with eight 16th-century Venetian masks.

Gabriele D'Annunzio (1863–1938) planted his ship (far left) in the grounds of Il Vittoriale. He used La Puglia to lead the occupation of Fiume (now Rijeka in Croatia).

Look north from Lake Garda and you see snow-capped mountains, while to the verdant west lie vines, and lemon and orange groves. But wander up through the backstreets of Gardone Riviera—a small 19th-century resort to the west—and you'll find a villa that's about as far from bucolic serenity as it's possible to get. The rambling Il Vittoriale was the home of Gabriele D'Annunzio: poet, soldier, fighter pilot, journalist, librettist, politician, novelist, womaniser, Fascist and above all, towering ego. Mussolini gave the villa to D'Annunzio in 1925, ostensibly to reward him for his patriotism, but in reality as a bribe to keep his wayward exhibitionism in check.

The villa was previously owned by German art critic Henry Thode before D'Annunzio converted it into an ostentatious monument to his achievements. Wander through the grounds and you will find evidence of his military prowess—a huge ship poking out of the hillside. This vessel, La Puglia, was used by D'Annunzio to lead the occupation of Fiume (now Rijeka in Croatia) after the Allies reneged on a promise to give it to Italy after World War I.

The main house is part Gothic fantasy, part exercise in mean-spirited tomfoolery. D'Annunzio was not a fan of sunlight, so once inside you have to wait a few seconds before the jumbled bric-à-brac of books, ceramics, leopard skins, and Buddhas emerge out of the gloom. There are two reception rooms: D'Annunzio kept one at a normal temperature for friends and the other stone cold for his enemies. Meanwhile the dining room is home to an expired tortoise which died of overeating—strategically placed to put off greedy guests.

Unsurprisingly, one of the villa's most prominent elements is the mausoleum. It's a huge three-tiered design based on Roman and Etruscan tombs, with an eternal flame burning in its crypt. At its apex lie D'Annunzio's remains, interred after a state funeral ordered by his old friend Mussolini.

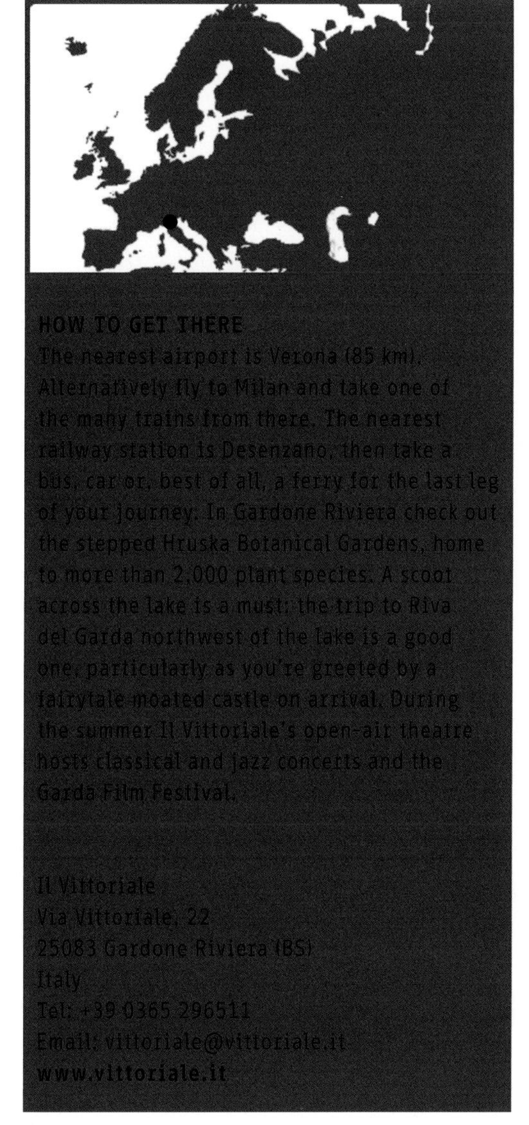

HOW TO GET THERE

The nearest airport is Verona (85 km). Alternatively fly to Milan and take one of the many trains from there. The nearest railway station is Desenzano, then take a bus, car or, best of all, a ferry for the last leg of your journey. In Gardone Riviera check out the stepped Hruska Botanical Gardens, home to more than 2,000 plant species. A scoot across the lake is a must; the trip to Riva del Garda northwest of the lake is a good one, particularly as you're greeted by a fairytale moated castle on arrival. During the summer Il Vittoriale's open-air theatre hosts classical and jazz concerts and the Garda Film Festival.

Il Vittoriale
Via Vittoriale, 22
25083 Gardone Riviera (BS)
Italy
Tel: +39 0365 296511
Email: vittoriale@vittoriale.it
www.vittoriale.it

From left to right: the Bedroom of Luisa Baccara, who accompanied D'Annunzio to Fiume; the Leper's Room (also known as the Pure Dreams Room) where D'Annunzio's body was laid out on the night of March 1, 1938; the Bedroom of Aélis Mazoyer, D'Annunzio's housekeeper.

"Remember that you are made of glass and I of steel." D'Annunzio's inscription on a mirror in his reception room, designed to give his enemies a cool reception.

Water/Glass House
Japan

This house is an exhibitionist's paradise, with almost every element made of glass, including the walls, floors, stairs, ceilings, handrails, and even the tables and the chairs.

"I want to erase architecture. That's what I've always wanted to do and it's unlikely I'll ever change my mind." Kengo Kuma (1954–).

Left: the transparent walkways, bathroom, and dining room (also following pages).

If you're the shy, retiring type, this villa is probably not the abode for you. The downside is that you can't throw ludicrous shapes to your favourite music unless you want your neighbours to ridicule you for months. The upside—uninterrupted views of the Pacific Ocean from within. You'll find the villa overlooking the Atami coast in east Honshu, Japan. It sits in an infinity pool, which creates the illusion that the whole structure is part of the sea. Spy it at night and the lounge appears to be floating on the ocean thanks to cleverly placed under-floor lighting.

The villa's origins can be traced back to Bruno Taut, an architect who fled Nazi Germany in the 1930s. Taut strongly believed in harmonious relationships between buildings and their environment, and he employed natural materials to build his own Atami coast home, the Zen-infused Hyuga Villa, to prove the point. It's no coincidence that a keen follower of Taut was commissioned to build a guesthouse next to his villa.

Kuma's Water/Glass House is something of a homage to Taut's "traditional meets modern" Japanese-style legacy. Rejecting industrial age architecture, Kuma creates experiences rather than just spaces, working hard to preserve a setting rather than impinging upon its natural beauty. He's also a master at blurring the division between structure and surroundings. Take a look his Kiro-san Observatory, which sits unobtrusively inside a mountain, or his Great Bamboo Wall House near the Great Wall of China (see p. 182). Water and light, key elements of traditional Japanese design, are all hallmarks of his work. This villa is the very embodiment of Kuma's aims—to make the surroundings the star.

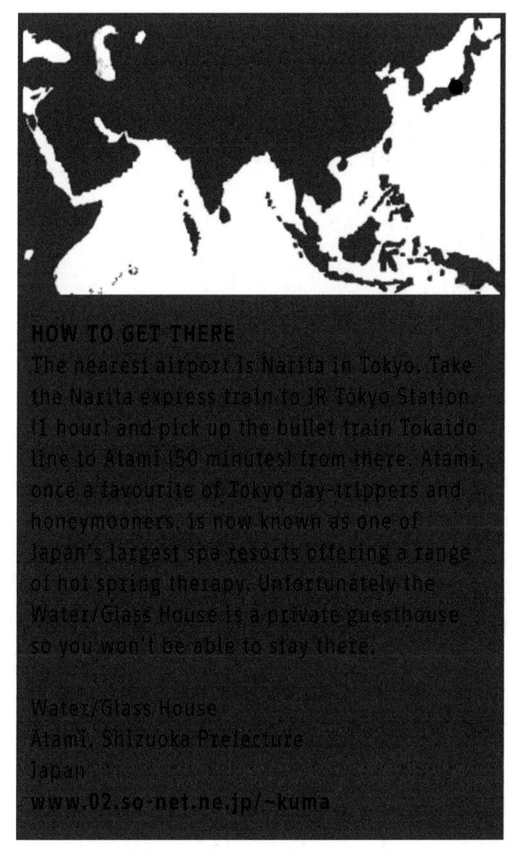

Casa Milà
Spain

Casa Milà is one of Barcelona's most famous landmarks. But when it started to rise from the pavement of the fashionable Passeig de Gràcia in 1906, it sparked a series of battles that rumbled on for 20 years.

"Everything comes from the great book of nature."
Antoni Gaudí (1852–1926)

Left: Casa Milà's seaweed-inspired wrought-iron balconies.

At six years old Antoni Gaudí was confined to his bed by rheumatic illness. He spent his convalescence devouring everything he could find on botany and zoology. The experience not only fuelled the architect's organic designs, it also instilled a resilient streak that was to prove vital for this project.

Businessman Pere Milà commissioned Gaudí to build a block of rental flats, complete with private residence, having been impressed by the architect's Casa Batlló—a house on Barcelona's Passeig de Gràcia. Soon Casa Milà was taking shape on the same street: an undulating, wave-like structure, featuring seaweed-inspired wrought-iron balconies, a polyp-populated roofscape, and a cavernous open-air core.

But construction was beset by a series of fiery disputes. Milà's wife, Roser Segimón, disliked the design and objected to spiralling costs. Standing his ground, Gaudí took the couple to court over his fee, won and gave all the money to the poor. The city government tried to halt construction, claiming the building was encroaching onto the pavement. City Hall also claimed it was too high and ordered the attic storey to be torn down. Gaudí refused to back down on both counts, and the authorities finally relented, allowing the block to be completed in 1910.

The fight was worth it. Casa Milà (otherwise known as the La Pedrera—"the quarry"—due to its hollow interior) is one of the finest examples of Modernista architecture, the Catalonian version of Art Nouveau inspired by the "return to nature" aesthetic of the Arts and Craft movement. Take your time in the building: wonderful organic details are everywhere, including in the doors, lifts, and Catalan-style vaults. There's also a plush early 20th-century private apartment and a good Gaudí exhibition. You may spy some lucky residents too, as there are still some privately owned flats in the building.

Pere Milà's wife had the last word in the dispute over design. When Gaudí died in 1926, Roser Segimón did away with his main floor entirely, replacing it with Louis XVI-style rooms. Casa Milà now has UNESCO status and was Gaudí's last private building.

"Artists do not need monuments erected for them because their works are their monuments." Antoni Gaudí.

Below and right: Casa Milà's "quarry" interior and roof terrace.

Brasília
Brazil

Is it a bird? Is it a plane? From the air it could be either, but on the ground there's no doubt: Brasília is the most audacious experiment in architectural modernism on the planet.

The National Congress building (far left) is designed so that the sun rises inside the "H" on Brasília's birthday, April 21.

Left: Brasília's chief architect Oscar Niemeyer (1907–).
Centre left: an aerial view of the city at dusk.
Following pages: the Avenue of the Ministries.

The idea was daunting. Create a new capital for Brazil to replace the crowded, coastal city of Rio de Janeiro. Build it on a vast plateau hundreds of kilometres from the nearest town and 600 kilometres from the nearest paved road. House half a million residents and kick-start an economic boom in Brazil's underdeveloped heartlands in the process.

The lofty ambitions of Brazilian president Juscelino Kubitschek called for a crack team. It came in the form of town planner Lucio Costa, architect Oscar Niemeyer, and landscape designer Roberto Burle Marx. The bond between Niemeyer and Costa was strong. They had built Rio's ground-breaking Ministry of Education building (1943), pulling in the talents of Le Corbusier in the process. And it was to Le Corbusier's modernist theories that they turned to create Brasília, conjuring up a city of segregated, function-led zones, communist-style egalitarian "superquadra" apartment blocks and sweeping roads, all in just three years.

The city was inaugurated on April 21, 1960. To many, though, it was deeply flawed. Costa's so-called Pilot Plan failed to factor in communal areas where denizens could freely mix. The dominance of the road system and the sheer distances involved made walking dangerous and impractical, and residential areas were criticised for being characterless and indistinguishable from each other.

But there are also legions of Brasília fans, who proclaim the city a monument of national pride and progress. Proponents also point out that Brasília has achieved its "economic catalyst" objectives—opening up the country's heartlands—and that recent additions such as new leisure facilities have done much to improve urban life.

Whoever you believe, it's an architecture fan's dream. Niemeyer's geometric government buildings are the highlight, residing in the cockpit of Costa's plane-style city plan. The president's Alvorada Palace, the futuristic cathedral, and the National Theatre are also all on the must-see list. Brasília was declared a UNESCO World Heritage Site in 1987. It has now sprouted satellite towns and is home to more than two million people. Bird or plane maybe, but certainly no dead duck.

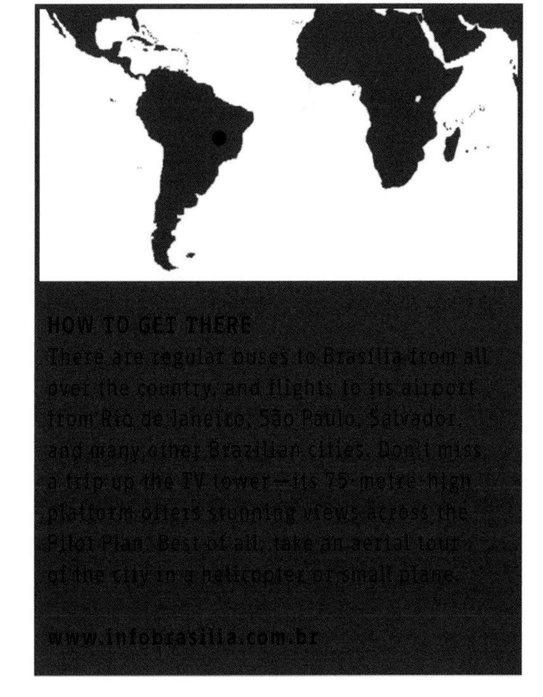

HOW TO GET THERE

There are regular buses to Brasília from all over the country, and flights to its airport from Rio de Janeiro, São Paulo, Salvador, and many other Brazilian cities. Don't miss a trip up the TV tower—its 75-metre-high platform offers stunning views across the Pilot Plan. Best of all, take an aerial tour of the city in a helicopter or small plane.

www.infobrasilia.com.br

Selfridges
England

Selfridges wanted to revive the glamour of the early days of the department store, and Birmingham sought a striking landmark. A combination of sheer determination and good old-fashioned chemistry delivered just that.

Far left: Selfridges' sheer membrane roof.
Left: the department store in context—a shimmering plateau in the centre of Birmingham.

In the late 1960s Jan Kaplicky was building his Prague architectural practice under an oppressive communist regime. Then in 1968 Russian tanks rattled into the Czech capital to crush the "Prague Spring"—the Czechoslovakian bid to introduce a liberal form of communism. The architect fled with just $100 to his name and, sensing Britain was about to become an architectural hotspot, headed for London.

Kaplicky went on to work with Richard Rogers, Renzo Piano and Norman Foster, but when he met Amanda Levete, an architect working for Rogers, sparks really began to fly. The duo's partnership built a reputation for striking retro-futuristic structures, underpinned by innovation, eco-ideology and cool glamour. After a 15-year personal relationship, the couple have now amicably separated but their creative partnership continues as principals of their practice, Future Systems.

Selfridges is Future Systems' biggest project to date. Completed in 2003, its vast organic form couldn't contrast more with surrounding modernist concrete efforts. A skin of 15,000 aluminium discs reflects changing weather conditions and light levels, and at night the building truly comes into its own, radiating blue light. The inspirations behind the design are all poetic—a curtain-style backdrop for the nearby church, a fly's eye and the chain mail dresses of designer Paco Rabanne are all cited. Head inside and it's almost an anti-climax to find conventional shops, restaurants, bars and cafés over five floors. There are no windows, but light pours in through the roof's sheer membrane to illuminate its two atria, served by escalators.

The building's success means Kaplicky and Levete are busier than ever, so it looks like we're going to see much more of the future very soon indeed.

HOW TO GET THERE

Birmingham's international airport is 13 km east of the city and there are frequent trains to the centre. If you're going by train get off at the city's New Street, Moor Street, or Snow Hill stations. By car you can park at Moor Street car park and walk over the footbridge. Selfridges is part of the city's re-developed Bull Ring shopping district and you'll find the city offers a good selection of restaurants, bars, galleries, theatres, shops, two cathedrals, and museums.

Selfridges
Upper Mall East
Bullring, Birmingham
B5 4BP
England
Tel: +44 8708 377 377
www.selfridges.co.uk

"The fluid shape and shimmering skin composed of thousands of aluminium disks provide an ethereal backdrop to nearby St Martin's church and the key elements of the interior are the dramatic roof-lit atrium criss-crossed by white sculpted escalators."

Judges of the Mies van der Rohe Award 2005, the European Union Prize for Contemporary Architecture.

Below: the department store is connected to Moor Street car park via a walkway.

Dhaka National Assembly Building
Bangladesh

Nathanial Kahn wasn't short of material when he made a documentary about his father's colourful life. But while films often fade from view, Louis I. Kahn's legacy lives on in Bangladesh.

"Architecture is the thoughtful making of spaces."
Louis I. Kahn (1901–74).

Far left: Kahn's National Assembly Building appears to float on the artificial lake. Left: the Dhaka skyline. Following pages: the building's sliced walls were designed to create a free flow of air, provide maximum protection from the rain and sun, and allow natural light to flood the building.

Born in 1901 in Estonia, Kahn emigrated to the United States at the age of four. He led an extraordinary life, juggling three different families (two mistresses bore him two illegitimate children) while designing a broad array of medical centres, synagogues, and student residences. Despite a prolific output he died a pauper, succumbing to a heart attack in a New York railway station in 1974.

The monumental National Assembly Building in Dhaka, Bangladesh, was Kahn's final project. It's a building of towering geometrical beauty. The vast structure features a circle of eight blocks surrounding an assembly chamber. It's classic Kahn—a sculpted brick and concrete composition infused with classical grace and natural light. What strikes you most is the tranquillity of the setting. Sitting among 80 hectares of parkland, gardens, orchards, lakes and fields, the building provides refuge from the crush and fug of the Bangladeshi capital. Kahn's structures are known for their sympathy with their surroundings. And as Dhaka is situated on the flood-prone delta of the Ganges and Brahmaputra rivers, Kahn set the whole building in an artificial lake. It took 18 years to build and was completed in 1982, eight years after the architect's death.

As for the origins of Kahn's modernist-meets-classical approach, you need to go back to his traditional Beaux-Arts training and his travels through Greece, Egypt, and Italy in 1950, where he studied and sketched classical architecture. Previously known as more of a theorist than a practitioner, his new hybrid style garnered his first major public commission—an extension for the Yale University Art Gallery, which opened in 1953. The project attracted major praise and he went on to design the Kimbell Art Museum in Texas and the Salk Institute in California.

In 1973, the Bangladesh government asked Kahn to continue his work in the area and design a community of houses and civic buildings to the north of the Parliament Building. The architect responded enthusiastically with plans for "a water architecture of bridges and crossovers" but died before his imaginative plans came to fruition.

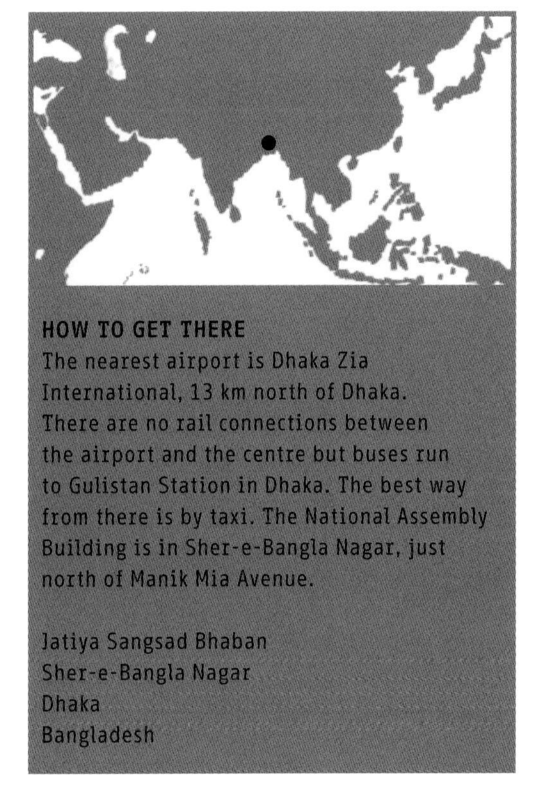

HOW TO GET THERE
The nearest airport is Dhaka Zia International, 13 km north of Dhaka. There are no rail connections between the airport and the centre but buses run to Gulistan Station in Dhaka. The best way from there is by taxi. The National Assembly Building is in Sher-e-Bangla Nagar, just north of Manik Mia Avenue.

Jatiya Sangsad Bhaban
Sher-e-Bangla Nagar
Dhaka
Bangladesh

Studio Weil
Mallorca

A ban on high-rise hotels guarantees inspiring views across to the sparkling Mediterranean from this Mallorcan town. So why does this artist's studio have no windows?

"It's a monumental building. You have a feeling that this is right. Everybody who comes loves it."
Barbara Weil (1933–).

Left and following pages: the studio's upper terrace, with the western staircase bisecting the structure.

You'd be hard pressed to find a better spot for a studio. Port d'Andratx is an upmarket fishing port and marina set among hills dotted with orchards and Italian-style villas. It is one of the most relaxed and picturesque places on the Balearic island of Mallorca. But you'll find precious few views from Barbara Weil's studio—the American painter and sculptor's studio is actually a sealed curving chamber, and it's virtually impossible to see in or out. It's the very antithesis of classic Mallorcan villa design. And this is entirely the aim, with the emphasis on the work and its relationship to its confines.

The man responsible is Daniel Libeskind—the architect chosen to design Ground Zero in New York, and someone whose work is characterised by the symbolism of memory. Weil and Libeskind worked closely together on the project: it was a natural partnership, particularly since much of Weil's work is concerned with the energy of inner spaces and creating emotions through basic forms. "I had a good feeling about him," commented Weil. "I could relate to him. We think the same way and have the same intellectual concepts."

Weil asked Libeskind to design the studio in 1998 and the two embarked on a five-year collaboration, producing a gallery and workshop, storage spaces and bathrooms, plus a landscaped garden. The result is a kind of "architecture meets art"—a quirky concrete slab, sliced by flights of stairs and switchback angles, and punctuated with concealed glass panels. Libeskind explains: "Working space, studio space and private spaces are withdrawn from the escapism of horizon and built into their own world."

The whole experience as you wander around Weil's kinetic works—from the lo-tech of carbon and pastel on paper to hi-tech fibreglass and automobile lacquer—is a remarkably positive one. With works and space working together to create something so moving, who needs bracing sea views?

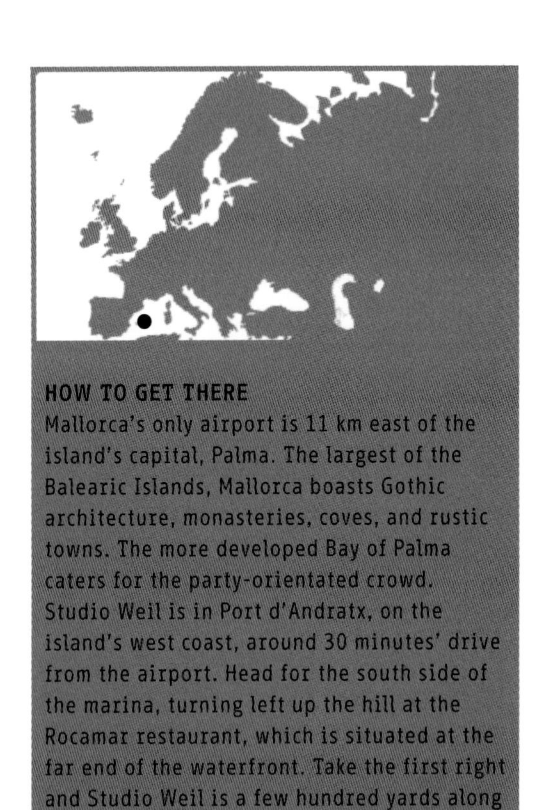

HOW TO GET THERE

Mallorca's only airport is 11 km east of the island's capital, Palma. The largest of the Balearic Islands, Mallorca boasts Gothic architecture, monasteries, coves, and rustic towns. The more developed Bay of Palma caters for the party-orientated crowd. Studio Weil is in Port d'Andratx, on the island's west coast, around 30 minutes' drive from the airport. Head for the south side of the marina, turning left up the hill at the Rocamar restaurant, which is situated at the far end of the waterfront. Take the first right and Studio Weil is a few hundred yards along on the left-hand side. Email Barbara Weil in advance if you want to visit the studio.

Studio Weil
CMO. San Carlos
Port d'Andratx
Mallorca
Spain
Email: weil@arrakis.es
www.studioweil.com

"The resulting structure, in which the external remains external, has the internal boring deeper into itself, creating an unexpected dialogue which every artwork carries within itself and every landscape forgets."
Daniel Libeskind.

Sámi Parliament Building
Norway

Traditionally a fishing and reindeer-herding people living on ice-bound slopes, the Sámi are the indigenous people of northern Norway, Finland, Sweden, and Russia. The Sámediggi is their hard-won parliament building.

Top left: inside the Sámediggi's plenary chamber, decorated with Hilde S. Pedersen's fresco. Opposite, bottom right: the design of the chamber was inspired by traditional Sámi tents. Right: the complex forms a semi-circle, redolent of a Sámi reindeer pen.

HOW TO GET THERE
The nearest airport is Banak Airport in Lakselv, 74 km north of Karasjok. There's no train option, so you have to take a bus or hire a car from there. Do check weather conditions before you go.

Sámediggi
Kautokeinoveien 50
9730 Karasjok
Norway
Tel: +47 7847 4000
E-mail: samediggi@samediggi.no
www.samediggi.no

If you trek across the ice fields and wind-scoured glacier tongues towards Karasjok in Norway, you'll come across this strange tepee-shaped building perched on a ridge around 500 kilometres north of the Arctic Circle. It's the home of the Sámi parliament, founded in 1989 to promote Sámi education, culture, commerce, and language, and represents a major breakthrough for one of the world's hardiest nomadic races.

Numbering around 85,000, the indigenous Sámi have their own language and culture, and have long protested at unfair treatment and forced cultural assimilation at the hands of Scandinavian governments. Both the Norwegian and Swedish governments have apologised for Sámi injustices, which include forcing indigenous people off their land and suppressing their language.

The Sámediggi was designed by Oslo-based architects Stein Halvorsen and Christian Sundby, and was opened by Norway's King Harald V in 1997. It draws on the design of a traditional Sámi reindeer pen to form a semi-circle housing 55 offices, conference rooms, auditorium, library, and archive. The focal point is its plenary chamber, built in the form of a huge *lavvu*—a Sámi tent decorated with an enormous gold-leaf and blue fresco designed by artist Hilde S. Pedersen.

Although the Sámediggi marks a breakthrough, the Sámi parliament still has some way to go. It can only act in a consultative role, advising the Norwegian government on issues affecting the country's largest ethnic minority. It can't yet pass new laws or change legislation, but it does have a reasonable annual budget and has the final say on Sámi primary schools, kindergartens, colleges, and cultural conservation projects. If typical Sámi resilience is anything to go by, it will only be a matter of time before its powers increase.

Beehive
USA

Can innovative buildings really revitalise run-down suburbs? To find out, head for Culver City in Los Angeles.

"The Beehive isn't a form. It's forms. And the forms change." Eric Owen Moss.

Left and right: the two-storey Beehive, one of a series of innovative buildings running in a diagonal strip across Culver City.

HOW TO GET THERE

The Beehive is 9.5 km from Los Angeles International Airport (LAX), and you'll be able to pick up a taxi from there. For up-to-the-minute bus options visit www.mta.net. Driving from the airport, take the 405 north, exit towards Washington Boulevard, turn left onto Sepulveda Boulevard, turn right onto Venice Boulevard and a final right onto National Boulevard. While you're there check out Moss's other LA buildings, which include the Kodak Complex, situated in the centre of LA off Jefferson Avenue. and La Cienega .

Beehive
8520 National Boulevard
Culver City
CA 90232
USA
www.ericowenmoss.com

In the early 1970s Frederick Samitaur-Smith owned a prune farm in Northern California. The trees died so he decided to develop the land, but he found he was chucking up characterless, boxy buildings wholly unsuited to their occupants. The area was the embryonic Silicon Valley, and his tenants were the creative entrepreneurs of the hi-tech boom. Determined not to make the same mistake with his next development, he set out to find someone who could design something truly innovative. That architect was Eric Owen Moss.

Samitaur-Smith and his wife Laurie bought pockets of land on a 23-hectare site in Culver City, a run-down suburb of Los Angeles, and set about planning a diagonal line of buildings to revitalise the area. Moss proceeded to design studios, offices, and performance space, his trademark deconstructionism evident throughout in the form of chopped, sliced, and idiosyncratic forms. These buildings are now occupied by some of the world's biggest brands including Kodak and Oglivy & Mather, property values have increased by 500 percent over ten years, and the development attracts swarms of design students every summer.

Completed in 2001, the two-storey Beehive is typical Moss—an artful reinvention of industrial space rendered in glass and sheet metal. Workers head through the reception and first-floor conference room to get to the roof terrace—a great place for meetings, with inspiring views across the city. Cleverly, the stairs also form the roof, following the shape of the exterior wall. Outside the building there are grassy mounds, landscaped for lunching and general lolling about.

Eric Owen Moss is the thinking man's architect, his interviews peppered with cerebral references to the likes of Kierkegaard and James Joyce. Such intellectual rationalisation is largely unnecessary: the regeneration of Culver City is proof enough that witty experimentalism beats bland industrial design hands down every time.

The Beehive's staircase forms the roof, and its meeting rooms are bathed in natural light.

Battersea Power Station
England

Protestors argued that this monolith would be a blot on the London landscape and damage surrounding parks and buildings. Some 70 years on, it's still one of the capital's most controversial icons.

Far left: Battersea Power Station across London's River Thames. J Theo Halliday designed the Art Deco interiors (left). Below: architect Sir Giles Gilbert Scott (1880–1960).

The largest brick building in Europe sits like an upturned billiard table on the bank of the river Thames, its four mammoth chimneys a striking feature of the London skyline. The project was contentious from the start. In the 1920s the British Parliament decided that London's chaotic plethora of small private power stations should be replaced by a single, homogenous structure. But protestors, who included the Archbishop of Canterbury, argued that the proposed leviathan would be a huge, polluting eyesore.

So it was Sir Giles Gilbert Scott—the famous ecclesiastical architect who was following in both his grandfather's and father's footsteps—to whom the government turned in 1930 to help create a harmonious "cathedral of brick". The resulting Art Deco power station opened in 1937, going on to burn more than a million tonnes of coal a year and generate almost a fifth of the capital's electricity supplies. The structure was not Scott's alone—while he styled the exterior, J. Theo Halliday was responsible for its overall shape and interiors, including its impressive Art Deco control room, parquet floors, wrought iron staircases and Italian marble turbine hall.

The power station was decommissioned in 1983, prompting another bout of controversy. A plan to turn it into a theme park fizzled out, but only after the listed building's innards had been ripped out and its roof removed. Exposure to the elements has hastened the damage and Londoners now split into two camps: some claiming the power station is a landmark to rival Buckingham Palace that should be preserved at all costs; others wishing the sorry industrial wreck would slide quietly into the river.

However, the story looks to have an upbeat ending: plans are underway to turn it into a £1.1-billion mixed-use development featuring shops, hotels, apartments, a theatre, and restaurants, due to open in 2008–9. And as for Scott, his designs are now regarded as some of Britain's most iconic, including the red telephone box and Bankside power station—now the home of Tate Modern art gallery.

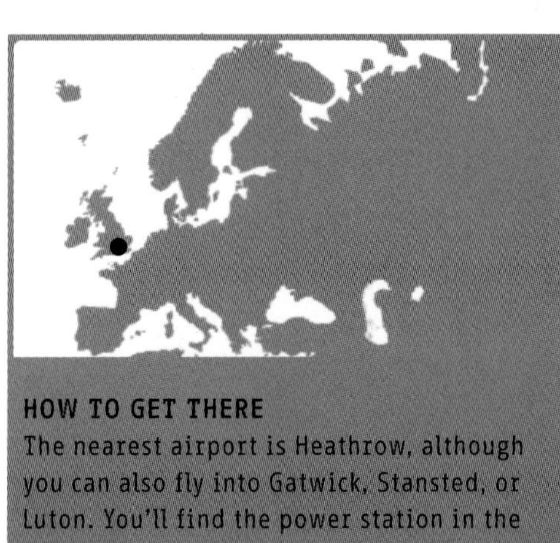

HOW TO GET THERE

The nearest airport is Heathrow, although you can also fly into Gatwick, Stansted, or Luton. You'll find the power station in the Borough of Battersea, near Westminster, Chelsea, and Kensington. The nearest underground railway station is Vauxhall. While you're in the area you should check out the Tate Britain gallery, which exhibits British art from 1500 to the present.

Battersea Power Station
Kirtling Street
London SW8 5BP
England
www.thepowerstation.co.uk

Guinness Storehouse
Ireland

When you next drink a pint of Guinness, several million people in 151 countries will be doing exactly the same thing. But there's one place where the creamy stout tastes undeniably better—the Gravity Bar at the Guinness Storehouse in Dublin.

"When I was sufficiently recovered to be permitted to take nourishment, I felt the most extraordinary desire for a glass of Guinness. I am confident that it contributed more than anything else to my recovery."
An extract from the diary of one of Lord Wellington's officers, after he was badly injured at the Battle of Waterloo in 1815.

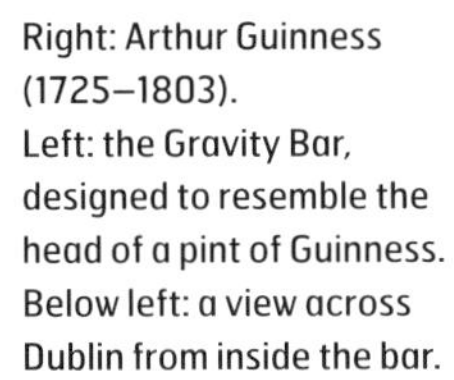

Right: Arthur Guinness (1725–1803).
Left: the Gravity Bar, designed to resemble the head of a pint of Guinness.
Below left: a view across Dublin from inside the bar.

The Storehouse is Guinness's Mecca, marking the spot where an optimistic 34-year-old Arthur Guinness took over a run-down brewery in 1759 and formulated a recipe for a new barley-infused brew. By the 19th century, Arthur's grandson was presiding over the largest brewery in the world.

The Storehouse was completed in 1904, the first steel-framed structure to be built in the British Isles. It was designed not by architects but by the brewery's engineers, who drew inspiration from the multistoreys of Chicago in the US. Originally the site of the fermentation process, it was converted by Dublin-based RKD Architects to house an excellent Guinness exhibition, opening in 2000. Your reward for exploring its six floors is a free sample of the black stuff on the top floor. Shaped like the neck of a pint, the Gravity Bar offers heady 360-degree views of the city, Wicklow Mountains, and the Irish Sea. The place has a constant buzz and, if you didn't know better, you'd think you'd stumbled upon a party in full swing.

The success of Guinness owes a great deal to clever marketing, but award-winning TV adverts and John Gilroy's classic toucan illustrations aside, you can't help but be drawn in by the romanticism of the brand. The globe-trotting stout succoured officers in the Battle of Trafalgar in 1805, made it to the South Pole in 1909, and can count British Prime Minister Benjamin Disraeli among its many fans. This buccaneering spirit can be detected from the drink's earliest days. In a dispute over the brewery's water supply in 1773, Dublin's sheriff threatened to cut off Arthur Guinness's vital river flow. Arthur grabbed a pickaxe from one of the sheriff's men and single-handedly faced the group off.

As for the famous claim that "Guinness is good for you", Arthur himself died in 1803 at the ripe old age of 78 having fathered 21 children. What more proof do we need?

HOW TO GET THERE

As Ireland's most popular tourist attraction, you'll have no difficulty in finding the Guinness Storehouse. It's situated in St James's Gate Brewery, a 15-minute walk from the city centre. There are numerous trams and buses to the brewery, and it's also a stop-off point on the city's "hop-on-and-off" sight-seeing bus routes.

Guinness Storehouse
St James's Gate, Dublin 8
Ireland
Tel: +353 (1) 408 4800
Email: guinness-storehouse@guinness.com
www.guinness-storehouse.com

Bodegas Ysios
Spain

Spain's Rioja territory conjures up images of dusty subterranean wine vaults and traditions going back centuries, but this ultra-modern bodega is in a world of its own.

"The language of geometry is as important as the language of structure." Santiago Calatrava (1951–).

Far left: Bodegas Ysios's towering atrium and rolling roofscape.
Bottom left: inside the bodega.
Left: the backdrop of the Cantabrian Mountains.
Following pages: a pool laps the bodega's cedar-clad exterior.

HOW TO GET THERE
The nearest airport is Agoncillo in Logroño, and there are buses every 30 minutes from Logroño centre to Laguardia, around 20 minutes away. Bodegas Ysios is 2 km from Laguardia. Pick up a taxi or better still stroll there in half an hour.

Bodegas Ysios
Camino de la Hoya s/n
01300 Laguardia
Álava
Spain
Tel: +34 945 600 640
Email: cac@adwes.com
www.laguardia-alava.com
www.bodegasysios.com

You'll find Bodegas Ysios near the walled town of Laguardia—a beautiful medieval hill town at the foot of the Cantabrian Mountains in northern Spain. Wine producer, Bodegas y Bebidas, wanted an iconic design that could hold its own against neighbouring wineries created by Frank O. Gehry and Rafael Moneo, and so turned to Santiago Calatrava. The Spaniard has a reputation for sublime (and often large-scale) geometrical creations including France's Bridge of Europe in Orléans and Bilbao's Sondica Airport.

Calatrava came up with a stunning 196-metre curve: a "rolling wave" aluminium roof mimicking the mountainous backdrop, and walls that evoke a row of barrels. The bodega is classic Calatrava—more of a sculpture than a building, it's both a work of art shimmering in the Basque sierra sun, and a cutting-edge space for making and selling wine.

So how did these eclectic skills come about? In 1968, a fresh-faced Calatrava left Spain to study at the Ecole des Beaux-Arts in Paris. He was a talented artist, but his timing was poor—the French capital was in the grip of rioting students and workers, protesting against unfair conditions under De Gaulle's government. So Calatrava returned to Spain, where he decided on a change of direction. He embarked on an architecture degree and went on to become a postgraduate in civil engineering. These hybrid talents have served Calatrava well, and he's now regarded as one of the world's most successful and progressive architects.

The bodega's highlights include its soaring atrium and balcony with views across the vineyard, and the tasting sessions where you get to sample the winery's award-wining output. Make sure you spend a few hours exploring Laguardia, too. The picturesque, pedestrianised town is packed with wine shops, gourmet restaurants, and cafés.

Carhenge
USA

Most of us would be happy with a memorial service and a low-key plaque. But when artist Jim Reinders' father died, ordinary commemoration just wasn't an option.

"Plane, loqui, deprehendi [to speak plainly is to be understood]."
Jim Reinders, creator of Carhenge, which is made entirely out of classic American cars.

In the summer of 1987, Jim Reinders invited 35 relatives to a remote corner of Nebraska in the US. Convening on a farm where Reinders' father had once lived, they proceeded to haul 38 cars into a circle. They then painstakingly welded a series of automobile lintels into place, and sprayed the entire installation stone grey. On the summer solstice the family stood back to admire the creation: Carhenge—a faithful replica of the ancient stone circle of Stonehenge in England. The family then held a memorial service, featuring poetry, songs, and a play written by the clan.

England's Stonehenge has perplexed historians, architects and engineers for centuries. Experts still aren't sure why the 5,000 year-old site was built, nor how prehistoric humans managed to lug the stone slabs—weighing between five and 45 tonnes—into place. Jim Reinders studied the stone circle during a stay in England, and when his father died Jim decided that a life-size replica would make the perfect memorial. As 45-tonne megaliths are not too plentiful in Nebraska, the artist chose to construct the monument out of the next best thing—classic American cars.

Reinders was a stickler for detail: he dug 56 "Aubrey Holes" at Carhenge, duplicating indents discovered at Stonehenge by antiquarian John Aubrey in the 17th century. The holes are believed to mark the first Stonehenge, built out of wood in around 3,000 BC. The Aubrey Holes make Carhenge a living work of art—they're now home to more than 30 installations and sculptures, including a giant salmon , and there are still a few holes yet to be filled. Artists keen to contribute should apply to the site's custodians, the Friends of Carhenge. Carhenge attracts some 90,000 visitors every year.

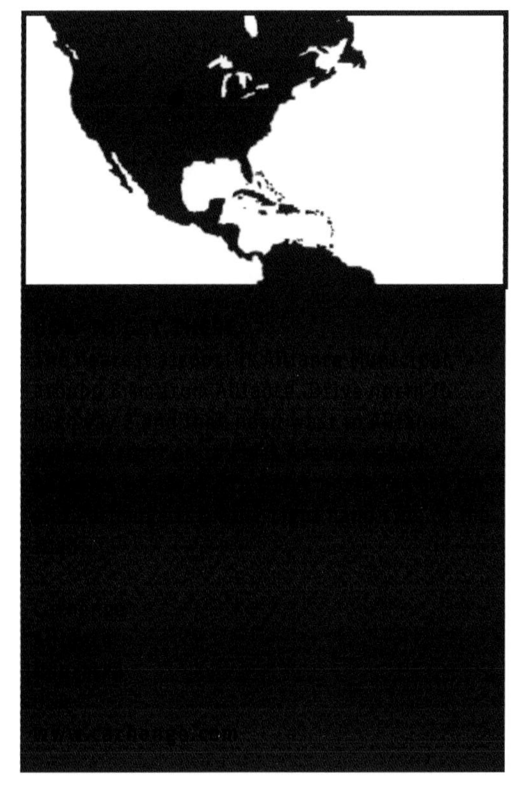

The Cymbalista Synagogue and Jewish Heritage Center Israel

"I was born in Germany, and I was standing there in 1938 when the synagogue in my home town was burnt down by the Nazis. I wanted to rebuild a synagogue, but in a place where it would stand forever." Norbert Cymbalista (1926–).

The synagogue's twin towers (right) represent the religious and secular communities of Israel. Following pages: inside the synagogue, which is clad with golden Tuscan stone and designed to let in light from above.

How do you persuade the religious and the secular to resolve their differences? Norbert Cymbalista's Synagogue and Jewish Heritage Center is working on it.

The Hebrew phrase for synagogue is *bet hakeneset*, which translates as "house of gathering". It's exactly what Norbert Cymbalista envisaged when he commissioned this project, but building a synagogue on a secular university campus proved harder than he thought. Tel Aviv University rebuffed the idea for 30 years, but then Cymbalista persuaded one of the world's best architects to design the centre and agreed to underwrite the whole project.

The building sits in the very heart of the university campus, housing a synagogue, auditorium, museum and study centre. "The idea is to get the very divided secular and religious segments of the Israeli Jewish population to meet in an academic environment, in order to start a constructive dialogue," commented Cymbalista, a Swiss property developer and governor of Tel Aviv University. The centre hosts regular symposia, lectures, conferences and meetings that aim to do just that. "Having all these activities including religious functions for Orthodox, Conservative and Reform Jews under one roof is considered unique and sensational," added Cymbalista.

Swiss architect Mario Botta proved the perfect choice. His designs are known for their cultural sensitivity, and are infused with geographical and historical references. Botta's work comprises two monumental towers measuring 17 metres wide and 13.5 metres high—symbolising a dialogue between the secular and religious. Little expense was spared on the materials: the exterior is clad in red stone from Italy's Dolomite Mountains, while the inside is adorned with golden stone from Tuscany.

Botta managed to meet an almost impossible brief—to create a space that was conducive to quiet prayer by being closed to the outside world, yet felt open and uplifting. The only light enters from above, so visitors automatically look to the heavens. Botta's A-list influences are also evident throughout: his trademark incorporation of natural light and dramatic geometrical space are both traits of his one-time teacher and colleague, the legendary modernist Louis I. Kahn.

"The success is astonishing", commented Cymbalista. "Participants come regularly from all over the country."

שויתי יהוה לנגדי תמיד

Le Palais Idéal du Facteur Cheval
France

Imagine a place where Christians, Muslims and Hindus can worship freely side-by-side. A French postman did and devoted 33 years to building it single-handed.

"What else is there to do when one is constantly walking in the same setting, apart from dreaming. To entertain my thoughts, I built in my dreams a magical place..."
Postman Ferdinand Cheval (1836–1924), creator of Le Palais Idéal.

Head for Hauterives, a small village in Southeast France, to find Ferdinand Cheval's madcap creation: a kind of Angkor Wat meets pharaoh kingdom, peppered with intricate Muslim and Christian iconography and guarded by a petrified menagerie of bears, boa constrictors, lions, and elephants.

The story of Le Palais Idéal is as bizarre as they come, particularly as its creator was a slight, ordinary *facteur* who could barely wield a trowel and knew nothing about architecture at the outset of the project. Cheval's daily postal round was a 32-kilometre trudge, and to entertain himself he often daydreamed of a "magical palace" spanning countries, religions, myths, and epochs. So when he tripped over a trove of beautiful stones one day in April 1879, he took it as a clear sign from nature to start building.

Cheval's first creations were pools and cascades, and before long he was labouring day and night. He acquired a sturdy wheelbarrow to cart pebbles and stones up to ten kilometres a day, and went on to shape a pharaoh's tomb, a cave of the Virgin Mary complete with angels, a staircase spiralling up nine metres, a Hindu temple, and three giant Egyptian figures.

Locals thought him mad, but word spread and foreign visitors were encouraging. "I was laughed at," Cheval wrote, "but as this kind of mental alienation was neither contagious nor dangerous, they didn't see much point in fetching the doctor and so I was free to devote myself to my passion in spite of it all." By 1912 the palace was complete. Despite being branded "a pathetic pack of insanities muddled in a boor's brain" by Ministry of Arts officials, the work was listed in 1969 and Picasso and André Breton were among its fans.

Cheval died in 1924. He had originally planned on being buried in one of his pharaoh's tombs, but settled for nearby Hauterives' cemetery. It was no ordinary plot—the postman was interred in the Tomb of Endless Silence and Rest, built by Cheval himself over eight years.

Pray

Ferdinand Cheval worked day and night to create a bizarre world of creatures, tombs, towers, and temples. Le Palais Idéal has been a source of inspiration for many artists including André Breton, Picasso, Jean Tinguely, and Max Ernst.

Glass Church
Jersey

A chance encounter on an idyllic island led to the creation of this sublime church interior, featuring a font, altar and angels designed by a world-famous glass artist.

Lady Trent (Florence Boot, 1863–1952) commissioned René Lalique to create this glass interior in honour of her husband Jesse Boot (1850–1931). The artist worked with local architect, A. B. Grayson, on the interior. The font is thought to be only full-sized glass font in the world.

It sounds like a fairytale. An ambitious young man took on the family business. Suffering from overwork, he headed to a sunny island to convalesce. There he met a bookseller's daughter, they married the following year, and together they built a successful business that afforded them every luxury. When the entrepreneur died, his wife commissioned a sublime monument in his memory, wrought entirely of glass.

It's a true story. The couple is Jesse and Florence Boot (Jesse founded the British pharmacy chain), and the commemorative work is by René Lalique, the finest Art Nouveau glass artist of his generation. The glass works are on Jersey, an island 23 kilometres north of the French coast. It's easy to see how Jesse and Florence fell in love here; to the north of the island are bracing cliff-top walks, to the south secluded sandy beaches, while inland is all rolling fields, where subtropical plants and vineyards flourish in the mild climate.

Florence Boot commissioned Lalique in 1932 and he spent two years on the project. It was a good commission for the Frenchman, who was keen to extend his repertoire of smaller decorative works such as perfume bottles, vases, and inkwells.

Many visitors trudge past the plain white façade of St Matthew's Church, oblivious to the treasures inside. It's an unremarkable building in the parish of St Lawrence, but the fine Art Deco panels of the church door offer some clue to the extraordinary interior. Inside there are angels, a huge cross, pillars, altar rail, font, and glass flowers, all with Lalique's trademark elegance and fine detail. Lalique created a unique formula for the work, producing a luminescent effect that gives the interior an uplifting glow.

Just to complete the fairytale, Jesse and Florence Boot didn't keep their wealth to themselves: they contributed to numerous projects in Jesse's native Nottingham, funding parks, almshouses, the hospital and the university. Florence's home island also benefited from their philanthropy—the Boots contributed £50,000 to build houses for Jersey's poor.

Nôtre Dame du Haut
France

A man who insisted that houses are "machines for living in" doesn't exactly sound like the spiritual type. So how did he end up designing this whimsical chapel?

Le Corbusier (Charles Edouard Jeanneret-Gris, 1887–1965) drew inspiration from the relationship between mother and child for this chapel.
Following pages: panels of coloured glass create a spectacular natural light show.

Attracted by stories of miracles, pilgrims have congregated on this hilltop in Franche-Comté since the 13th century. The previous chapel was destroyed by German bombs in 1944 and its replacement, built between 1950 and 1955, is a playful sculptural form with extremely thick walls and an immense skyward-pointing roof. Step inside and you'll find a spartan, curved interior. Light is the star of the show: shafts pierce the space through deep windows, some filled with coloured glass. The overall effect is dramatic, creating an atmosphere guaranteed to move religious and secular alike.

Le Corbusier studied the Catholic faith intently when designing the chapel. Likening the relationship between church and worshipper to that of mother and child, he created a broad entrance to embrace the visitor. He also cracked the hardest part of the brief: the congregation can swell to thousands on feast days, so he devised an external chapel space to accommodate the crowds, placing the Virgin high above the altar so it could be seen from both inside and out.

So how does this design square with Le Corbusier's rather hard-nosed architectural theories? As a progenitor of the International Style, he favoured mass production, rationalisation and standardisation—great for creating sterile space, hopeless if you want a cohesive community with any character, say his critics. But perhaps the chapel isn't a radical step change for Le Corbusier after all, more a natural evolution of his highly structured style. And with softer parabolic forms replacing cold-blooded geometry, he managed to create a more positive, free-flowing aesthetic.

For a possible answer, look to the man himself. According to Le Corbusier, "architecture is the masterly, correct and magnificent play of volumes brought together in light." Visit this chapel, and you can see what he means.

Pray

The Golden Temple
India

The Sikhs' holiest shrine is a sublime refuge, open to all visitors regardless of faith or nationality.

The Golden Temple sits on a promontary in the complex's Amrit Sarovar (pool of nectar).

Sexual and social equality, a focus on tackling everyday problems, and a rejection of ritual for ritual's sake—ideas that seem progressive for many religions, even today. So imagine how radical these beliefs were some 500 years ago, when Guru Nanak founded Sikhism.

Born of a Hindu family in the 15th century, Nanak was keen to quel the antagonism between Hindus and Muslims, arguing that religion should unite rather than divide. More than 20 million people now follow his teachings and those of the nine gurus that came after him. For a first hand insight head for Amritsar—a frenetic and polluted city in the Punjab in northern India. You have to battle through streets clogged with rickshaws, bazaars, and thronging crowds to reach the Golden Temple, an enclave of beauty and quiet contemplation amid the madness.

The temple complex marks the spot where the fourth guru, Ram Das, founded Amritsar upon discovering a pool with healing properties. The fifth guru, Arjan Dev, laid the temple's foundation stone in 1588. Appropriately the complex comprises a mix of Hindu and Muslim architecture, and features a central Amrit Sarovar (pool of nectar), 68 holy shrines, the Akal Takht (the seat of the Sikhs' governing body) and a community canteen, which feeds around 10,000 people every day.

The temple has four entrances representing the openness of the faith, while its dome, reputed to be clad with 100 kilogrammes of pure gold, is designed in the shape of an inverted lotus flower pointing earthwards to signify the religion's focus on worldly issues.

You have to leave your shoes at the entrance when you visit; padding around the marble walkways induces a spirit of slow-paced calm. Cross the promontory and step inside the temple proper and you'll find a cramped interior, with carved wooden panels and silver and gold inlay. Here musicians chant devotional songs and accompany a recital of the Guru Granth Sahib, the Sikhs' holy book, read by priests in three-hour shifts.

Despite this tranquillity the history of the temple isn't blood-free. It was rebuilt several times during the 17th and 18th centuries after being destroyed by Muslim armies. Tragedy also struck in 1984, when the complex was occupied by fundamentalists fighting for a Sikh homeland. Prime Minister Indira Gandhi ordered an attack, which killed 200 soldiers and trapped 2,000 others inside the complex. The bungled mission led to the assassination of Gandhi by her Sikh bodyguards.

Pray

Far left: a terrace in the temple building. The temple houses the Sikhs' holy book, the Guru Granth Sahib (near left), which is read by priests in shifts.
Below left: the temple is said to be clad with 100 kg of pure gold.
Right: thousands of pilgrims file through the temple's ornate interior every day.

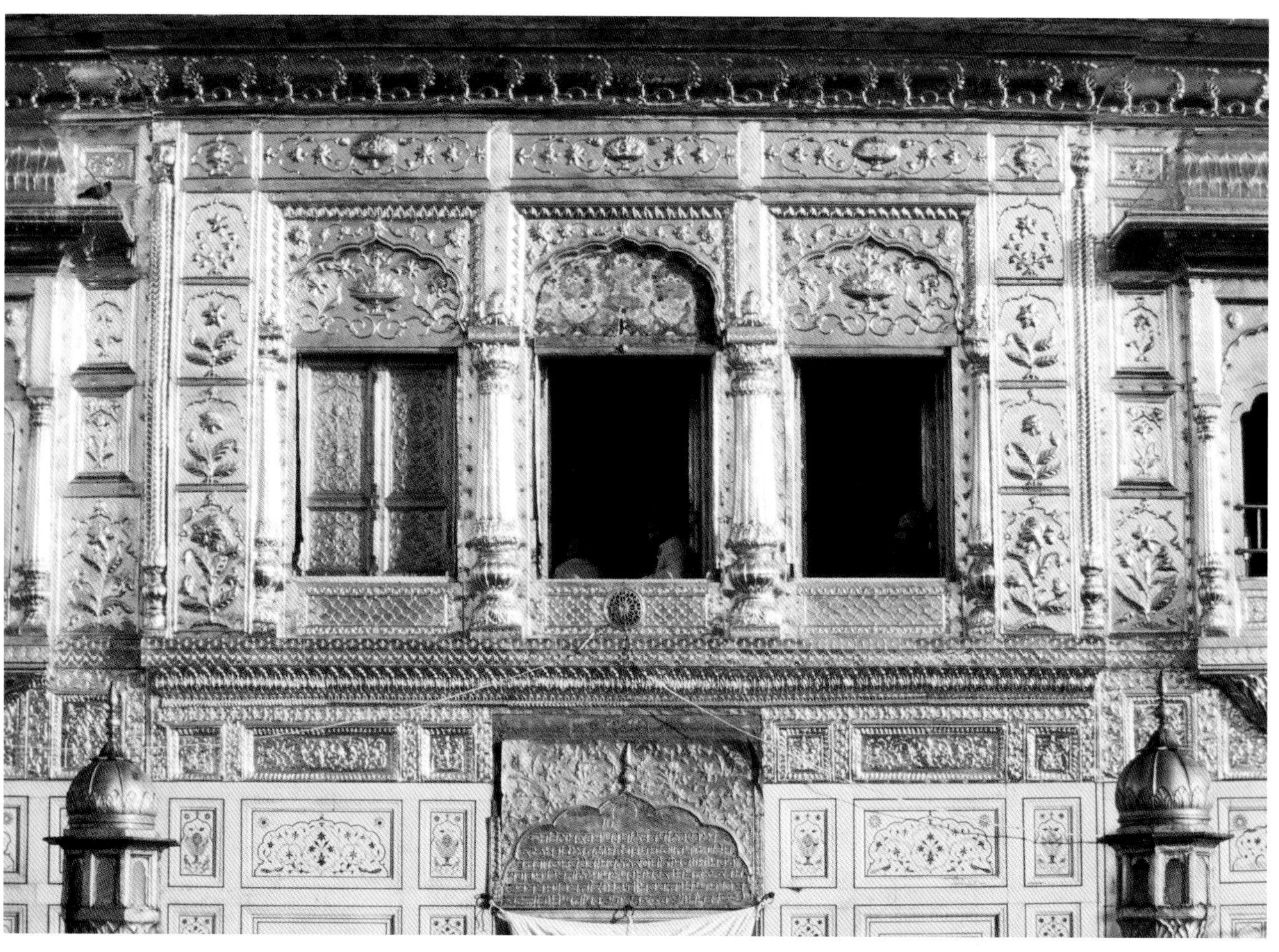

Chapel in Wieliczka Salt Mine
Poland

There's everyday religious devotion and then there's piety on an epic scale. Three Polish miners score pretty highly in the latter category as they spent nearly 70 years creating an underground chapel entirely made of salt.

Guided tours start at the head of the Danilowicz Shaft (right) and cover two kilometres—just a fraction of the mine's 300-kilometre network. The Pieskowa Skala Chamber (bottom left) is one of the most beautiful parts of the route.

HOW TO GET THERE

You'll find Wieliczka Salt Mine 10 km east of Krakow on the E40 road. If you're using public transport, take a train to Krakow Main Railway Station (Dworzec Glowny) and pick up a connecting train or minibus from there. Be prepared for the 380-step descent to the first level of the mine, and you should wear some warm clothing as temperatures are around 14 degrees Celsius. An original miners' cage lift zips you back to the surface at the end of your trip. The return journey is not for the claustrophobic, but is mercifully over in seconds. Tours are available in several languages.

Kopalnia Soli 'Wieliczka' Trasa Turystyczna sp. z o.o.
ul. Danilowicza 10
32-020 Wieliczka
Poland
Tel: +48 12 278 73 02
Email: turystyka@kopalnia.pl
www.kopalnia.pl

Head deep into the Wieliczka Salt Mine and you'll find the miners' creation: a 54-metre-long, 10-metre-high cavern hewn out of walls of green salt. Under the light of three huge crystalline sodium-chloride chandeliers you'll find painstakingly carved bas-reliefs depicting the Last Supper and numerous other Biblical scenes.

Miners had been holding Catholic services in the mine for centuries, due to the sheer inconvenience of leaving their subterranean confines to pray. But it took Jozef Markowski to create a truly impressive place of worship. He started the Chapel of Saint Kinga in 1895, carving the altars and pulpit 100 metres below the surface. His younger brother Tomasz then picked up the hammer and chisel between 1920 and 1927, before Antoni Wyrodek spent another 36 years adding detailed bas-reliefs to the chapel walls.

The Wieliczka Salt Mine dates back to the Middle Ages, and galleries burrow 327 metres below ground and extend to a network of 300 kilometres. Thankfully today's guided tours are limited to around two kilometres, and take in 20 carved chambers and a vast salt lake. Visitors walk in the footsteps of some high-profile characters, including Copernicus, Goethe, Chopin, and local Polish hero, the late Pope John Paul II.

Salt underpinned the local economy for centuries. A valuable commodity used to preserve meat and fish and tan hides, it was an essential ingredient of gunpowder and was even used as currency. Polish monarchs quickly tapped into the value of the salt mines, which by the 14th century were generating more than 30 per cent of the state's annual income.

The Wieliczka Salt Mine is now a UNESCO site and one of Poland's biggest tourist attractions, hosting weddings, banquets and orchestral concerts—the latter well worth attending as the mine boasts near-perfect acoustics. And if you find ending your epic tour in a gift shop a little inappropriate, at least you can pick up a reminder of how it all started: the shop sells small replicas of one of the chapel's most moving sculptures—a solitary miner, carrying an oil lamp.

Left and below: the Chapel of Saint Kinga, where even the chandeliers are made of salt. Following pages: the Weimar Chamber's underground lake was formed when the floor flooded with brine in the 1960s.

Esplanade—Theatres on the Bay
Singapore

This arts complex, situated where the Singapore River flows into the sea on Marina Bay, is all front—literally.

"We wanted it to be an assemblage of all-enveloping, all-embracing 3-D forms."
Michael Wilford, architect of Esplanade—Theatres on the Bay, which sits between the high rises and the harbour of Singapore's Marina Bay.

When Michael Wilford won the competition to design the Esplanade, he packed his bags and set off on a fact-finding trip around Southeast Asia. The area's thatched long houses—where numerous community facilities can be found under one roof—provided the inspiration for the complex. Built ostensibly to give international visitors a reason to stay an extra night or two in Singapore, it comprises two giant glass domes housing three state-of-the-art theatres, a 1,600-seater concert hall, and several outdoor performance spaces. The whole structure is wrapped in an organic mesh, redolent of Southeast Asian textiles.

"It's unique in that is has no back and four fronts," commented Wilford, who collaborated with Hong Kong-based DP Architects on the project. "The biggest challenge was making a building that responded to all sides—including the harbour, shopping district, and the high rises looking down from above."

Wilford was also keen to make the centre's public areas as transparent as possible—affording visitors inspiring views over the city and the bay both night and day. But at around 130 kilometres from the equator, high temperatures and heavy rainfall posed a major challenge for his glass designs. The solution lay in a double-skin exterior incorporating timber and banana leaves, and aluminium "scales" to reflect the intense heat. The shields can be set at different angles depending on the position of the sun, keeping internal temperatures steady and views unsullied. The scales have earned the complex its "durian" moniker—the durian is a Southeast Asian fruit with a thorny skin.

Visitors will find it hard to fault the acoustics: sound and theatre experts were engaged even before the architects came on board. It was also designed to be a truly international cultural space, doing justice to both western and eastern art forms from full symphony orchestras and pop bands to Indian music, Chinese opera and Malay performance. The $339-million complex opened in 2002 with a programme featuring 70 productions from 22 countries.

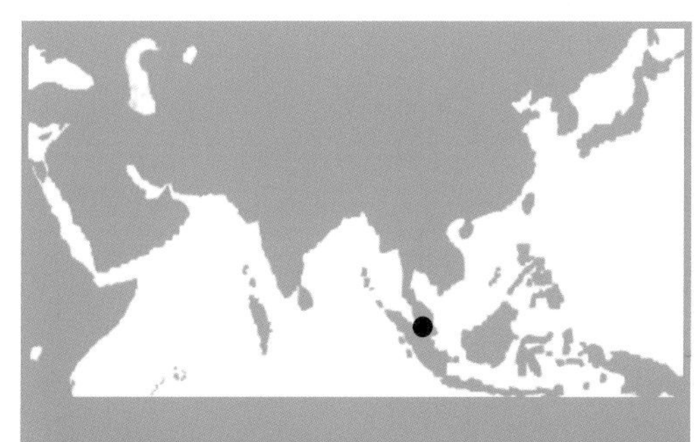

HOW TO GET THERE

The nearest airport is Changi International, 22 km away. Once you've reached the city, the most stylish way to get to the Esplanade is by river taxi—they run from 9 a.m. to 10.30 p.m. You can also get there by bus, or catch a train to City Hall Mass Rapid Train Station, ten minutes' walk away. If you're driving, the Esplanade has a handy underground car park.

Esplanade–Theatres on the Bay
The Esplanade Co. Ltd.
1 Esplanade Drive
Singapore 038981
Tel: +65 6828 8222
Email: boxoffice@esplanade.com
www.esplanade.com

"Singapore is no longer the cultural desert it used to be." Graham Hayward, executive director, Singapore's International Chamber of Commerce, *Financial Times*.

The building sports adjustable aluminium scales (below) to reflect the intense heat and ensure optimum natural light levels, while the concert hall (right) ensures top-quality acoustics for a broad cultural programme.

"I want the biggest conservatories in the world," Tim Smit told his team of architects. Some £86 million and 100,000 plants later Tim got his way, creating a world-class eco-enclave in the process.

"I want Eden to give people licence to ask questions." Tim Smit (1954–).

Left, top: Tim Shaw's Rites of Dionysus sculptures in the Warm Temperature Biome.
Left, below: inside the Humid Tropics Biome, the largest conservatory in the world.

Following pages: Eden's famous self-cleaning biome panels, designed by Nicholas Grimshaw and Partners.

The Eden Project lies in an old china-clay pit in south Cornwall, a world away from the low-slung granite towns and golden sandy beaches of the surrounding countryside. Covering an area equivalent to 35 soccer pitches, it was conceived as a "living theatre" designed to tell the story of the human race's dependence on plants. The star attractions are two huge geodesic biomes, bubbling out of the hillside like giant frogspawn. In the humid tropical conservatory visitors can explore a full-height rainforest with banana, rubber, cocoa, mahogany, and teak trees, while the temperate house is filled with vines, olive trees and citrus trees plus other plants from the Mediterranean.

The man responsible for Eden is Tim Smit, a former music producer and composer who decided on a radical career change after a string of hit records in the 1980s. "I thought that that was what I needed to make me happy," said Tim. "But then I realised it's about the journey. Getting there is a real depression." Drawing on his archaeology and anthropology degree, Tim became fascinated with the potency of plants and their positive effects on people, and embarked on project that, in theory at least, should have no end.

After months of searching Tim found a disused clay pit near St Austell and work started in 1994. It was a mammoth task involving shifting nearly two million tonnes of earth and importing thousands of rare plant species from around the world. But even 100 days of continuous rain failed to dampen the construction team's enthusiasm and Eden opened to glowing reviews in 2001. Nicholas Grimshaw and Partners designed the stunning biomes, standing 55 and 35 metres high.

A visit to the Eden Project is proof that a man armed with vision and an uncompromising attitude, backed by a strong team, can realise even the most outlandish idea. Make sure you spend some time outside the conservatories, exploring plants suited to the Cornish climate as well as Eden's sculptures, exhibition spaces, and new education centre. The latter is an architectural homage to the Fibonacci sequence—nature's growth blueprint that creates the patterns of overlapping scales found, for example, in pinecones and pineapples.

Smit and his crew are already planning a third, semi-arid biome, so it looks like "getting there" won't be an issue for Tim for a long while yet.

HOW TO GET THERE

The nearest airport is Newquay. The Eden Project is well served by public transport and you can buy a combined train, bus transfer, and admission ticket. The nearest train station is St Austell, and buses run from here and many other nearby towns including Newquay, Truro, and Falmouth. If you're coming by car you'll find the Eden Project 6.4 km east of St Austell and there are signposts directing you from there. The best way is to arrive by bike: the Eden Project is on the UK's National Cycle Network.

The Eden Project
Bodelva, St Austell
Cornwall PL24 2SG
England
www.edenproject.com

Yabani
Lebanon

Once known as the Paris of the Middle East, Beirut is emerging from a 15-year civil war to become a thriving, cosmopolitan capital once again. But one architect is keen not to forget the past.

"Yabani is the product of a scenario that attempts to describe a fraction of a society living in marvellous denial." Bernard Khoury.
Far left and left: Yabani contrasts with the surrounding buildings of Damascus Road.
Below: diners are seated in a collective circle.

Life in Beirut in the late 1970s and 1980s meant spending a great deal of time underground, escaping the shells and bullets of the civil war. It's this experience that inspired Lebanese architect Bernard Khoury to build Yabani, a stark tower and subterranean retreat situated on the former border between east and west Beirut.

Khoury's Yabani building is part monument, part celebration of post-war freedom. Comprising two storeys below ground and a 14-metre-high steel tower, it houses a Japanese restaurant, club and two Oriental sunken gardens. The architect chose a politically potent spot for his work: it's close to Damascus Road, where surrounding buildings still bear the scars of shelling. It also represents Khoury's strong views on the city's development: "I would describe 'post-war' Beirut as a fantastic but terrifying product of western influences gone out of control," commented Khoury. "Yabani is not a 'postcard' building, its architecture attempts to reflect another urban reality."

Visitors get around the building using a transparent lift, which whizzes to the restaurant at level minus one or to the club at level minus two. Dining is a surreal and collective experience—guests are seated in a circular formation following the curve of the building, forcing everyone to observe each other at close quarters. Relief is provided by natural light and sky views courtesy of glass ceiling panels, which actually sit at ground level.

When visiting, be prepared for a two-part experience: the surrounding ruins are still squatted by refugees, so although you can party and dine insulated from the country's past, arriving and leaving makes it impossible to ignore the war, and the enduring gap between the haves and the have-nots.

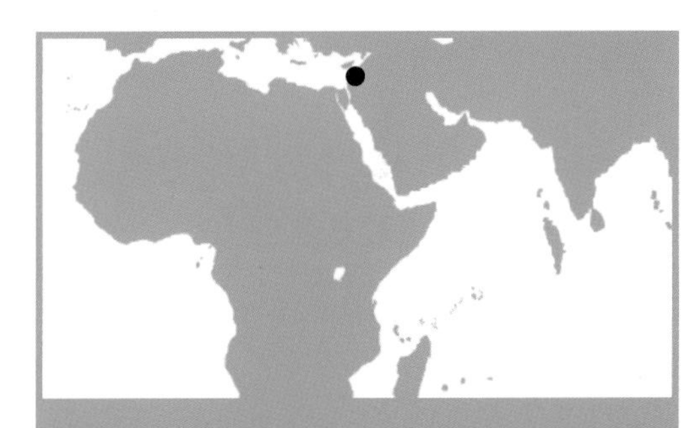

HOW TO GET THERE

The nearest airport is Beirut International, 9 km from the city and a 15-minute drive from the city. The best way to get to Yabani is by taxi. The entire city centre has been re-built, and cobbled streets, pavement cafes, and a decent nightlife should warrant a few days' stay. While you're there you should check out Khoury's B018—a bunker-style nightclub that opens its roof to allow dancers to gyrate in the night air.

Yabani
Damascus Road, Achrafieh
Beirut
Lebanon
Tel: +961 1 211113
www.bernardkhoury.com

Kunsthaus Graz
Austria

Moveable cities, "plug-in" towns, servile robots —all ideas that seemed perfectly reasonable to optimistic designers of the 1960s. But what if, after 40 years, not one of your psychedelic visions had actually been constructed?

"It was an important achievement in terms of vindicating myself. Writing and drawing is one thing, but once you start actually building, then you occupy a different piece of history....It vindicates a whole lot of other things that would otherwise have been written off."
Peter Cook (1936–)

Left: natural light pierces Kunsthaus Graz through strategically-placed nozzles, while its plexiglass skin changes colour according to the mood and time of day.

HOW TO GET THERE
Graz airport is situated 10 km south of the city, and there are frequent buses and trains to the centre. A taxi will take around 20 minutes. The best way to get to Kunsthaus Graz is to take tram lines 3 or 6 from Graz Central station. Austria's second-largest city is a popular short break destination with a strong cultural offering including classical music festivals, churches and museums.

Kunsthaus Graz
Landesmuseum Joanneum
Lendkai 1
8020 Graz
Austria
Tel: + 43 316/8017-9200
Email: info@kunsthausgraz.at
www.kunsthausgraz.at

A sceptical world has proved no obstacle to Peter Cook, who persevered until the doubters saw the error of their ways. The result is Kunsthaus Graz—a "work of art that houses works of art" designed by Cook in collaboration with Colin Fournier under the duo's Spacelab partnership.

The globular "friendly alien" was built to celebrate the city's Cultural Capital of Europe status in 2003, and languishes on the banks of the River Mur, bulging 60 metres across and housing 11,000 square metres of flexible event and exhibition space. Visitors are sucked into the belly of the beast via a slow-moving travelator to find floors with few clearly defined walls or ceilings—this really is meant to be a journey into the unknown. Natural light floods through nozzles along the creature's upper side and, best of all, it changes colour and tone thanks to an "intelligent" plexiglass skin.

To understand the significance of Kunsthaus Graz you have to go back to Archigram, an influential group of architects and creatives co-founded by Cook in 1961. The group challenged modernist architectural thinking, arguing that buildings shouldn't adhere to the accepted "form follows function" model, but instead harness technology to evolve according to changing user needs and the environment. Although the group was highly productive and influential, none of its ideas made it past the drawing board intact.

Kunsthaus Graz represents a jubilant victory for Archigram ideology in general and Cook in particular. The Fournier and Cook partnership has managed to incorporate technology, environmental sensitivity, and a degree of malleability that would have made the founders of Archigram proud. But then, Kunsthaus Graz doesn't quite live up to the duo's original vision. They planned that the blob would change shape, and even swivel to follow the sun. A fully realised Archigram vision, unsullied by compromise? If Cook has anything to do with, it's only a matter of time.

Jameos del Agua
Lanzarote

If you were to design your ultimate fantasy retreat, the chances are it would look something like Jameos del Agua.

"When I returned from New York, I came with the intention of turning my native island into one of the more beautiful places in the planet, due to the endless possibilities that Lanzarote had to offer." César Manrique.

Left: Jameos del Agua boasts the perfect tropical pool.

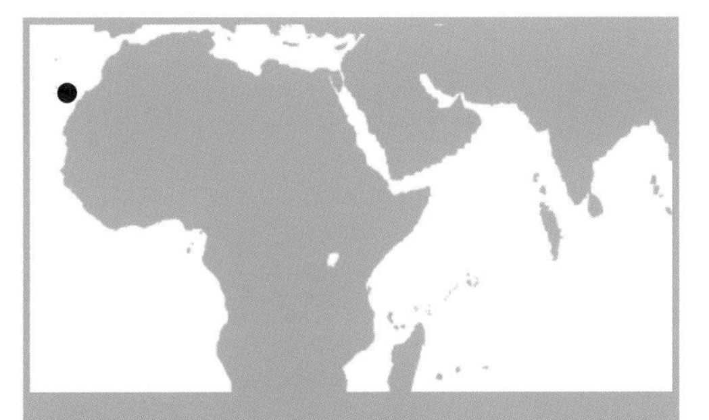

HOW TO GET THERE
Jameos del Agua is situated to the north of Lanzarote, near the fishing village of Arrieta. Buses from the island's capital of Arrecife are infrequent, so the best way to get there is by car—a mode of transport of which Manrique would not have approved. You have to pay to get in so make sure you take a few euros. While you're in the area check out the nearby laval cavern of Cueva de los Verdes: it's home to a huge natural concert hall and a great optical illusion, which visitors have to promise to keep secret. Lanzarote's only airport is 6 km southwest of Arrecife.

Jameos del Agua
Lanzarote
Canary Islands
Tel: + 34 928 84 80 20
www.fcmanrique.org

This subterranean hideaway exudes 1960s' cool—a Barbarella-meets-Bond-baddie lair complete with ice-cool pool, restaurant and, just for good measure, a 600-seater concert hall. It sits in a cavernous lava grotto complete with natural lake, formed when seawater burst inland after a massive volcanic eruption. And where better than a retro-chic bar to ponder the achievements of Jameos del Agua's creator, César Manrique?

Manrique is regarded as nothing short of a god by fellow Canarians. On his death the Lanzarote-born painter, sculptor, town planner, and public artist left a multifaceted legacy of performance spaces, restaurants, and landscapes that now feature high on every visitor's "must-see" list.

Manrique's key moment came in the mid-1960s. The artist had spent many years away from the Canary Islands, first studying in Madrid, then travelling the world and ending up in New York in 1964, where he mixed with artists such as Warhol, Pollock, and Rothko, and exhibited at the Guggenheim Museum. He returned to Lanzarote in 1966, but was appalled at the creeping development driven by the island's nascent tourist industry.

Manrique founded a campaign to preserve the Canaries' natural and cultural heritage, kick-starting numerous initiatives including a ban on roadside billboards and high-rise buildings to an ambitious artistic programme. His overarching aesthetic theme was Art-Nature/Nature-Art—in essence, development in harmony with the natural environment. Jameos del Agua is the perfect embodiment of Manrique's philosophy. There's even an edifying volcanic exhibition, which counterbalances the place's more frivolous playboy elements.

Manrique would certainly have been happy with his final achievement: his lobbying helped secure Lanzarote's UNESCO status, awarded a year after he was killed in a car accident in 1992.

Jameos del Agua's natural lake (far left and below) is home to rare blind crabs (*Munidopsis polymorpha*), while its rock-hewn auditorium (far left, bottom) offers excellent acoustics.

Longleat Maze
England

If you're after English eccentricity and a beard you could lose a badger in, the seventh Marquess of Bath is probably your man.

"The number of my wifelets or girlfriends is always being wrongly reported. I've only had 75—no, make that 74."
Seventh Marquess of Bath, Alexander Thynn (1932–).

Far left: Longleat's hedge maze—one of the biggest in the world.
Left: Longleat is set in parkland landscaped by "Capability" Brown.

Alexander Thynn represents blue blood at its eccentric best: his tally of unofficial wives—he calls them "wifelets"—numbers more than 70, and he's devoted the last 30 years to daubing colourful murals on the walls of his country seat. He played chess for the House of Lords, and his prolific creative output has included several novels, portraits, sonnets, songs, and essays with titles such as "Death, festival and the pantheistic ethic" and "A charter for world government".

But don't be fooled. These headline-grabbing antics belie a canny, commercial mind. The marquess' Longleat estate comprises 3,600 hectares of rolling Wiltshire parkland and an impressive Elizabethan residence—home to his family for nearly 500 years. His father opened the house to the public in 1949 to defray maintenance costs; the seventh marquess now presides over a successful tourist attraction featuring a hugely popular safari park.

For many, the main event is Longleat's hedge maze. It's one of the largest in the world and a typical Thynn project, a canny combination of mystical indulgence and astute money-spinner. Laid out by British designer Greg Bright in 1975, the maze comprises more than 16,000 English yews and features 2.72 kilometres of winding pathways. Make sure you leave plenty of time when you visit—most people take an hour and a half to complete it and there are frequent rescue missions at closing time. There are also six wooden bridges, affording you frustrating glimpses of the centre throughout your ramble.

The maze's success has prompted a flurry of labyrinth construction on the estate. It has now been joined by the Sun Maze and Lunar Labyrinth, King Arthur's Mirror Maze, and the Love Labyrinth, based on Botticelli's *Primavera* painting and the Garden of Love at Villandry, France.

Those intrigued by the marquess' life story can peruse the first few exhaustive volumes of his autobiography on his website (www.lordbath.co.uk). You'll have to wait a while for the unexpurgated version though—the marquess has vowed not to publish the full work until all those mentioned are deceased.

HOW TO GET THERE

Longleat is situated to the west of England between Bath and Salisbury. Warminster is the nearest train station, approximately 8 km away, where you'll find taxis to take you to the estate. If you're driving, Longleat is just off the A362 between Warminster and Frome.

Longleat
Warminster, Wiltshire
BA12 7NW
England
Email: enquiries@longleat.co.uk
www.longleat.co.uk

Guggenheim Museum
USA

Frank Lloyd Wright survived huge personal turmoil to become one of America's greatest sons. This museum is the architect at his provocative best.

Frank Lloyd Wright (1867–1959).

The museum is situated opposite Central Park (right). Its floors spiral upwards, forming an open rotunda over six levels (left and following pages).

HOW TO GET THERE

The museum is easily accessed by subway or bus. If you're driving, there are parking spaces within walking distance at Impark Parking on 40 East 89th Street. You'll get a discounted rate if you show your parking ticket at the museum's membership desk.

Guggenheim Museum
1071 Fifth Avenue
at 89th Street
New York, NY 10128-0173
Tel: + 1212 423 3500
Email: boxoffice@guggenheim.org
www.guggenheim.org

It's the stuff of not one but several lives. During his 91 years Frank Lloyd Wright designed 1,141 projects, more than 500 of which were built. He revolutionised architecture with a free-flowing, organic aesthetic, designing religious buildings, hotels, skyscrapers, offices, bridges, and a string of pioneering private houses. Meanwhile his personal life swung between tranquil and tragic. In 1909 he left his wife and their six children for a married woman, who was later butchered to death in their home by an axe-wielding cook. In the 1920s extravagant overspending left him bankrupt. But from the 1930s, during the latter third of his life, bursts of creativity led to some of his biggest commissions. Stability reigned.

It was with characteristic self-belief and resilience that Wright took on the Guggenheim in 1943. Hilla Rebay, a German baroness, had spent years amassing an impressive collection of European paintings for Solomon R. Guggenheim, the heir to a mining fortune. And now they needed an exhibition space that did justice to the work.

The commission became Wright's consuming passion: a 16-year endurance test featuring fiery run-ins with New York's building department and constant design revisions. But even World War II and his benefactor's death failed to scupper the project and construction finally started in 1957. Keen to avoid the traditional museum design of interconnected rooms, Wright set out to create a series of flowing, interdependent spaces. The result is a remarkable organic rotunda made entirely out of concrete, with a fountain at its core. Once inside, you follow the building's curved form via a gently spiralling ramp to explore six gallery floors, each hosting some of the world's best 19th- and 20th-century art, including Brancusi, Kandinsky, Miró, Picasso, and Van Gogh.

The museum is testimony both to Wright's nature-inspired approach and his dogged experimentation with cutting-edge materials. The architect believed buildings should form naturally from their settings and drew particular inspiration from the Transcendentalists such as Henry Thoreau and Ralph Emerson, who believed that absolute truths lay in nature.

The museum was predictably controversial: some artists even complained that the design might overshadow the work. Wright rebuffed the doubters with his usual aplomb: "On the contrary, it was to make the building and the painting an uninterrupted, beautiful symphony such as never existed in the world of art before." Wright died just months before the Guggenheim Museum opened in October 1959, his bullish self-belief intact until the end.

The Rock Garden of Chandigarh
India

India, 1973. Government workmen are hacking through the jungle and stumble upon a surreal, secret garden. Thirty years later it's the second most popular tourist attraction in the country.

"I find it ironical that people pay to see and even appreciate the same waste they discarded from their houses as refuse. The lesson it taught me is that all things created by Him [God], even garbage, have a higher purpose in life."
Nek Chand (1924–).

The Rock Garden features more than 2,000 sculptures (left and following pages), and a waterfall (bottom left).

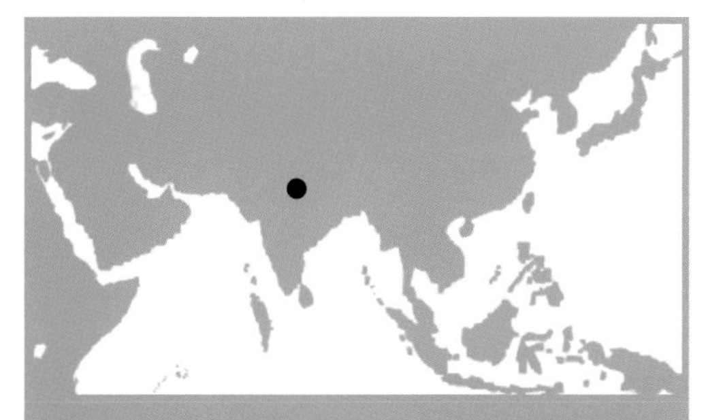

As a child Nek Chand often dreamed about a fantasy kingdom. So when he had the dream again in his early 40s he decided to start work. In 1965 the highways inspector found a remote spot on the outskirts of Chandigarh—the Le Corbusier-designed capital of the Punjab—and set about creating a small clearing. He then built a series of makeshift sculptures, but being a firm believer in recycling, and vehemently opposed to the practice of burying rubbish, he used scrap materials harvested from recently bulldozed villages. The secret project was illegal—it occupied government land and Chand didn't have planning permission—so he worked at night, extending the garden to five hectares over the next eight years.

When the garden was discovered, the government's response confounded all expectations. Instead of halting the project it awarded Nek Chand a salary and offered him the help of 50 workers to continue his work. Nek Chand had no landscape design or architectural training, but that didn't stop him expanding his garden to some 10 hectares with more than 2,000 sculptures of broken crockery, neon strip lights, cycle tyres, glass, bitumen drums, electrical fittings, plumbing, and industrial slag.

The garden is now recognised as an outstanding example of Outsider Art, ranking alongside France's Le Palais Idéal du Facteur Cheval (see pp. 94-95) and Watts Towers in Los Angeles. You'll find Chand's earliest work in the garden's first section, which features figurative sculptures of deities, birds, soldiers, monkeys, tigers, and battalions of figures. The second area is devoted to entertainment and play: a surreal playground with mosaics, courtyards, arched walkways, waterfalls and canal, miniature village, and open-air theatre.

Now in his 80s, Nek Chand is working on what will probably be the final phase of development. Life-sized horses and camels are being built on a broad walkway leading to the exit, and children will be encouraged to climb over the creatures by way of a final fantasy fling. Never has a load of rubbish been so much fun, or so enlightening.

HOW TO GET THERE

Chandigarh's airport is about 12 km east of the city and offers connections to Delhi, Amritsar, and Leh. There are also frequent buses and trains between Chandigarh and major Indian cities. If you're travelling from the northwest use the Kalka–Shimla railway—a narrow-gauge toy train that winds from the foothills of the Himalayas through the Punjab plains. The 96-km trip takes around 5.5 hours, but it's worth every second. The train terminates 26 km from Chandigarh so you have to switch trains at Kalka for the final leg. The garden is in the north of the city in sector 4. Le Corbusier's capital is very diffuse, so take a rickshaw or be prepared for a long walk from the station.

The Rock Garden of Chandigarh
Sector No. 4 Chandigarh (U.T.) India
Tel: +91 172 740 645
www.nekchand.com

The Nek Chand Foundation
1 Watford Road
Radlett, Herts. WD7 8LA
England
Tel: +44 (0)1923 856644
Email: info@nekchand.com

Sapporo Dome
Japan

Heavy snowfall and Siberian winds are hardly ideal ingredients for a stadium. But add a floating pitch and it's a whole different ball game.

Hiroshi Hara (1936–).

Opposite: Sapporo Dome has been likened to a giant computer mouse or silver oyster.
Its moveable turf soaks up the sunshine (left).
Seating is configured in a single tier to guarantee good views for all (right).

HOW TO GET THERE

The nearest airport is Chitose Airport, offering shuttle buses that drop you close to Sapporo Dome. The airport is half an hour from Sapporo city centre by train. From Sapporo centre take the Toho subway line to Fukuzumio Station (7.5 km, 11 mins). The stadium is about 10 minutes' walk from there. The Sapporo Dome offers tours on certain days. Sapporo has a good art park, botanical gardens, Sapporo beer museum, and a historical village with 50 buildings. Sapporo hosted the 1972 Winter Olympics, so don't miss the Winter Sports Museum.

Sapporo Dome
1-3 Hitsujigaoka
Toyohira-ku
Sapporo City
Hokkaido 062-0045
Japan
Tel: +81 (0)11 850 1020
www.sapporo-dome.co.jp

In 1996, Hiroshi Hara received a competition brief that would make most architects laugh or just bury their head in their hands. Sapporo City, on Japan's northernmost island of Hokkaido, wanted an all-weather stadium capable of hosting rock concerts, exhibitions, baseball, and crucially, high-profile soccer games for the 2002 World Cup tournament. The design had to withstand sub-zero temperatures and heavy snowfall, and incorporate real turf as FIFA, soccer's governing body, insisted all games had to be played on natural grass. Grass will not survive if permanently covered, but the sheer weight of winter flurries made a retractable roof an unlikely option.

It was the perfect project for Hara. As one of Japan's top architects, he's known for his love of innovative technology and for his theories of buildings as "states of flux". He responded with a masterstroke of lateral thinking: if the roof couldn't move, the pitch would instead. He designed two arenas: one outdoor with natural turf; the other a giant silver oyster housing artificial turf and protecting up to 43,000 spectators from winter winds. For soccer games in bad weather, the outdoor pitch could simply glide indoors on a bed of compressed air, hovercraft-style.

His extraordinary proposal won the judges over 7-1. Football fans were soon witnessing the spectacle of an 8,300-tonne slice of grass floating into a stadium in two hours flat. And as per the brief, configurable seating meant the indoor arena could be transformed from a diamond-shaped baseball field to a soccer field or concert stage as required. Even the seating was innovative: an egalitarian single-slope stand inclining at 27 degrees to ensure good views for all spectators.

The home ground of the Consadole Sapporo football team sits in a 31-hectare park of gardens and playing fields. Built on former sheep pasture and still surrounded by farmland, Haka's organic "sports garden" has now been dubbed Hiroba ("meeting place") by locals. To appreciate the scale of the place when you visit, check out the roof-top observatory, which at 53 metres above ground level gives you a bird's-eye view of the inside of the stadium, downtown Sapporo, and probably the most expensive piece of the turf in the world.

Tjibaou Cultural Centre
New Caledonia

If you're looking for paradise on earth, New Caledonia is a pretty safe bet. These South Pacific islands offer stunning mountains, white beaches, towering pines, and the chic, cosmopolitan capital of Noumea.

"We need to reconcile modernity and technology with nature and tradition."
Renzo Piano (1937–).

"We, the Kanaks, see it as a culmination of a long struggle for the recognition of our identity; on the French government's part it is a powerful gesture of restitution."
Marie-Claude Tjibaou (widow of Jean-Marie Tjibaou) on the cultural centre .

The centre runs along a promontory ridge (left and overleaf) and boasts impressive research facilities (far left).

The Tjibaou Cultural Centre is an extraordinary sight, perched on a peninsula between a calm lagoon and the rolling Pacific. But leaf through the history books and you'll find an altogether less idyllic image—one of colonial exploitation of indigenous people and a bloody quest for independence. The centre is dedicated to the culture of the Kanaks, oppressed by the French after Napoleon III set up a military regime there in 1853. It's named after Jean-Marie Tjibaou, who championed the Kanak cause and was assassinated in 1989 while negotiating autonomy from the French government. He was killed by a pro-independence hardliner who believed Tjibaou had compromised Kanak rights by signing a power-sharing agreement with France.

Architect Renzo Piano wanted to design a space that did justice to the Kanaks' struggle, but that also looked forward and helped build a positive post-colonial future. He created ten conical houses, sporting huge timber ribs which shoot up to 28 metres skywards. The design is a nod to a traditional Kanak dwelling, but falls short of perfect imitation as the architect was keen to avoid gimmicky replication. The structures are designed to withstand earthquakes and cyclonic winds, and their natural ventilation system even harnesses prevailing trade winds. This traditional-meets-modern, experimental-yet-functional design is typical Piano.

Inside the houses reside an exhibition space, an auditorium and amphitheatre, research centres, a conference room and a library, plus studios for traditional activities such as music, dance, and sculpture. A pathway runs through the park, winding around ceremonial grounds and residences for visiting artists, academics and students. Walking through the series of unfinished and finished, enclosed and open spaces leaves you feeling protected yet close to nature—natural elements such as light, wind, and vegetation making it a living, breathing space.

The Tjibaou Cultural Centre was opened in 1998 by Lionel Jospin, the French Prime Minister of the time. It was financed by the French government.

HOW TO GET THERE

The nearest airport is Tontouta International, which offers regular shuttle buses to Noumea (45 km). The Tjibaou Cultural Centre is located about 7 km east of Noumea on an island promontory at Baie de Tina. From Noumea take a Blue Line public bus (15 mins), taxi (10 mins) or Le Petit Train (up to 1 hour).

Tjibaou Cultural Centre
Rue des Accords de Matignon, Tina
BP 378 - 98845 Noumea Cedex
New Caledonia
Tel + 687 41 45 45
Email: adck@adck.nc
www.adck.nc

Reef HQ
Australia

Without a tank, goggles and flippers, getting close to the sharks of Australia's Great Barrier Reef is almost impossible. But visit Townsville and you can scare yourself witless without ever leaving dry land.

"We needed to publicise the glory of the Great Barrier Reef so that people would appreciate it and voluntarily protect it because we could never do it as a police programme." Graeme Kelleher (1933–).

Right: the giant tanks from above.
Left: visitors can immerse themselves in marine life by walking through a transparent tunnel, and can talk to divers through an intercom.

HOW TO GET THERE
The nearest airport is 6 km from central Townsville, and there are taxis and frequent shuttle buses into town. Reef HQ is located in a complex in the centre of Townsville's entertainment precinct and is a short walk from its ferry terminals. The complex also houses a cinema showing 3D films of the reef and a branch of the Queensland Museum. Situated in the dry tropics of Northeastern Australia, the area boasts 300 days of sunshine a year and is a good base from which to explore the outback, islands, rainforests, and the Great Barrier Reef itself.

Reef HQ
2–68 Flinders Street
Townsville QLD 4810
Australia
Tel: +61 7 4750 0800
Email: info@reefHQ.com.au
www.reefhq.com.au

Reef HQ, situated next to Townsville harbour, comprises two enormous tanks, the biggest being the world's largest living reef aquarium—a 2.5-million-litre behemoth housing a natural ecosystem. Reef life is here in abundance: 120 species of fish dart among sea urchins, anemones, giant clams, sea cucumbers and more than 100 types of coral. Step through a transparent tunnel to come face to face with reef sharks, stingrays and turtles, where you can talk to scuba divers through an intercom. A model replica of the bow of the SS Yongala, consigned to the deep of North Queensland by a cyclone in 1911, completes the Davy Jones' Locker experience.

Reef HQ was conceived by Graeme Kelleher. As chairman of the Great Barrier Reef Marine Park Authority in the early 1980s, Kelleher sought a way to protect the world's richest marine habitat while raising awareness of its importance and fragility. The answer lay in an education centre featuring a mini-version of the Great Barrier Reef—the real thing lies just off shore, curling 2,300 kilometres along the northeast coast of Australia. The project also resulted in the founding of a new ferry terminal and the headquarters of the Great Barrier Reef Marine Park Authority.

Work on Reef HQ started in 1985, with the creation of a huge concrete basin. As mining in the Marine Park is strictly forbidden, materials had to be carefully sourced: 700 tonnes of coral substrate came from a stockpile left after harbour development on a nearby island, while collecting 200 tonnes of sand involved returning large organisms to the lagoon floor. The formula worked, with coral polyp creating pristine outcrops, branches, and caves in a kaleidoscope of colours. Importantly, Reef HQ is unsullied by the pollution and overzealous diving that has damaged some parts of the reef proper.

Reef HQ opened in 1987, in time to mark the bicentenary of the British settlement of Australia the following year. It benefited from a AU$4.9 million upgrade in 2002 and now attracts more than 100,000 visitors a year.

The Minack Theatre
England

As you watch the waves crashing against the rugged Cornish coast and breathe the Atlantic air deep into your lungs, you understand why this exact spot was chosen.

"The Minack Theatre has the—perhaps unique—distinction of providing discomfort and some degree of danger for everyone." Rowena Cade, correcting a local drama critic's claim that the Minack was "Europe's most beautiful open-air theatre" in *The Cornishman*, 1954.

Rowena Cade (1893–1983) decorated the seating (far left) with play titles and Celtic designs using the tip of an old screwdriver and cement. Billy Rawlings and Tom Angove worked with her to build the theatre, which overlooks Porthcurno beach (left). Minack means "rocky place" in Cornish.

The Minack Theatre is perched on the edge of a cliff overlooking Porthcurno, a remote white-sand beach on Cornwall's south coast. What makes the venue so extraordinary is that its existence is down to one woman, Rowena Cade. She designed and co-built the entire theatre, devoting two thirds of her life to creating one of the most atmospheric performance spaces in the world.

The story starts in 1931. A drama group was looking for an open-air venue to host its next production—Shakespeare's *The Tempest*. Cade, the daughter of a Derbyshire cotton-mill owner, had moved to Cornwall in the 1920s and had built a house for herself and her mother on the Minack peninsula. Being a keen drama fan, she willingly offered up her cliff-top garden. But there was a problem: there was nowhere for the audience to sit. Rising to the challenge, Rowena enlisted the help of two Cornish craftsmen and spent six months building a simple stage and primitive seating. *The Tempest* ran through the summer of 1932 with car headlights and the moon providing the illumination.

The play was such a success that Rowena realised she couldn't stop there. Over the next half-century Rowena and her workers toiled in all weathers to create terraced seating, a car park and access road, and steps up from the beach. Even World War II failed to stop her, as the theatre was commandeered to defend the south coast. While restoring the venue at the war's close, Rowena managed to put the gun post to good use, converting it into the theatre's box office. The open-air theatre now accommodates 750 people and hosts a busy summer programme ranging from Shakespeare to modern drama and musicals.

Rowena Cade died in 1983, just short of her 90th birthday. She left plans for the next stage of development—a roof to be used in inclement weather. Just for once, it seems Rowena hasn't got her way.

HOW TO GET THERE

The Minack is near Land's End, at the very far west of Cornwall in the UK. The nearest airport is Newquay. The theatre is an hour's drive from Truro and 20 minutes from Penzance: leave plenty of time when travelling as Cornwall's narrow lanes can get very congested. There's a good visitors' centre, but for a performance bring something soft to sit on and don't forget to pack some warm clothes for evening shows—the Cornish air can get very chilly. Your perfect day would be to spend a few hours on the beach and then walk up to the theatre for an afternoon or evening performance. Shows run from May to September.

The Minack Theatre
Porthcurno, Penzance
Cornwall TR19 6JU
England
Tel: +44 (0)1736 810181/471
Email: info@minack.com
www.minack.com

Ngorongoro Crater Lodge
Tanzania

If you've never watched a herd of wildebeest sweep across the floor of a collapsed volcano while having your back scrubbed, well frankly you haven't lived.

"It is impossible to give a fair description of the size and beauty of the crater, for there is nothing with which one can compare it. It is one of the wonders of the world."
Professor Bernhard Grzimek, *The Serengeti Shall Not Die*.

Far left: the lodge's design is based on local mud and stick dwellings.
Left: Maasai warriors on the rim of Ngorongoro Crater.

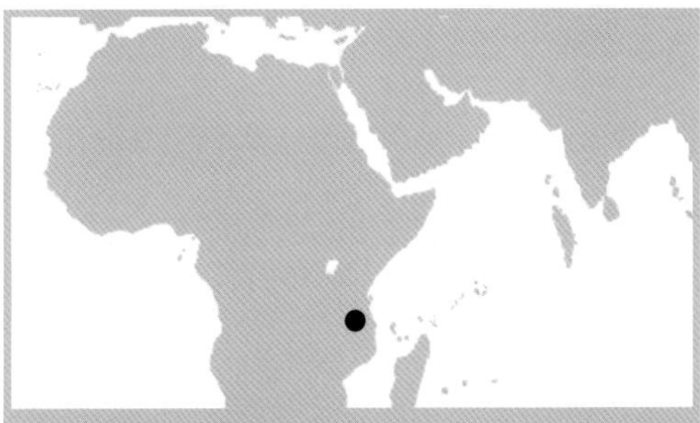

HOW TO GET THERE
Ngorongoro Crater Lodge is accessible by scheduled flight from Arusha Airport, followed by a 2.5-hour road transfer.

Ngorongoro Crater Lodge
CC Africa, Private Bag X27
Benmore, Johannesburg 2010
South Africa
Email: safari@ccafrica.com
www.ccafrica.com

Perched 600 metres up on the lip of the Ngorongoro Crater in Tanzania, this safari lodge gives you a bird's-eye view of some of the world's most endangered beasts, all from the comfort of your hot tub.

The place is built on worthy foundations: it was constructed and is run by Conservation Corporation Africa, which promotes eco-tourism and conservation, and aims to help sustain rural communities and habitats through managed tourism.

The lodge is loosely modelled on local Maasai villages: architect Sylvio Rech drew his inspiration from the tribe's traditional mud-and-stick "manyatta" dwellings, but don't be fooled—beneath the grass roofs you'll find a brand of luxury rivalling the world's most exclusive retreats.

Each of the 30 suites boasts exotic interiors adorned with carved wood, silk drapes, Persian rugs, chandeliers and tribal art, and all afford stunning views across the 23-kilometre-wide caldera and the Serengeti below. Service is top-notch too: a masseur is on hand to sooth away the rigours of the safari, while a private butler will run your bath and stoke the home fires. Such luxury, combined with a generous flinging about of rose petals, makes the place a honeymoon hotspot and the perennial favourite of the upmarket travel press.

If you want to get a closer look at the animals, safari tours will take you into the crater, now a UNESCO World Heritage site. Its grasslands and forests are home to black rhino, black-maned lions, flamingos, leopards, hippo, zebra, and elephants, plus a wealth of flora and bird life.

Going further afield you'll notice that the lodge's opulence couldn't contrast more with the habitat of the locals. The Ngorongoro Conservation Area is home to 42,000 Maasai people who live in dung huts surrounded by briar fences, herding cattle to survive.

A rustic exterior belies a luxurious interior—complete with hot tubs and chandeliers.

The Pineapple
Scotland

It's not often you get the chance to sleep in a giant pineapple—particularly one that's linked to the rise of George Washington, the American war of independence and the decimation of indigenous Indians.

"The experience of actually living in such a building is so much more rewarding than merely visiting. Hooray for the Pineapple, prickly and proud. Farewell, old fruit." Comment in the visitors' book.

The 11-metre-high Pineapple crowns the summerhouse on the Dunmore estate. It was commissioned by John Murray, the fourth Earl of Dunmore (1732-1809).

Thanks to the Landmark Trust, you and three friends can spend a few nights in this fruit's cosy confines, which can be found near Stirling in Scotland. The retreat comes complete with open fire but does away with unnecessary features such as internal doors—you have to go outside to walk from room to room.

The story of the Pineapple began in 1774. The British governor of Virginia, the fourth Earl of Dunmore, had just led the colonists to victory over Native American tribes. He was hailed as a hero by the Virginian elite, including one George Washington. But just two years later the Earl's stock plummeted catastrophically. Fearing the colonists were becoming too autonomous and were plotting to overthrow British rule, he confiscated their gunpowder and dissolved the Virginia legislature. A battle ensued and he was forced to flee the US, hotfooting it back to his Scottish estate with the war of independence ringing in his ears.

Lord Dunmore had heard that sailors often spiked a pineapple on their gatepost to announce their return home. His famous sense of humour still intact, he commissioned a suitable advertisement to mark his own homecoming—an 11-metre-high stone pineapple to cap his summerhouse. It was no coincidence that the pineapple was also an extremely exotic and expensive fruit, thus making it a fitting symbol for a prime mover of the British Empire.

Much to the amazement of the locals, the giant fruit sprouted atop the Earl's Palladian pavilion in 1777, proudly overlooking his walled garden. It is painstakingly designed, and to prevent frost damage there are even separate drainage outlets for each of the delicately carved stone leaves. The identity of the architect is unknown.

The Earl's career didn't end in Virginia. He was appointed governor of the Bahamas from 1787 to 1796—the perfect climate for a pineapple lover.

HOW TO GET THERE

The Pineapple is situated on the Dunmore estate in central Scotland, 0.8 km northwest of Airth, and 12.8 km southeast of Stirling. Driving is the easiest option, although you can take a train to Stirling, Larbert or Falkirk stations and pick up a taxi from there. The Pineapple is a holiday residence only, so you can't visit ad hoc. Contact the Landmark Trust to book your stay.

The Pineapple
Dunmore
Scotland
Tel: + 44 (0)1628 825925
www.landmarktrust.org.uk

Burj Al Arab
United Arab Emirates

Anti-capitalists look away now—this Dubai hotel is 321 metres of towering, mind-boggling indulgence.

"We decided that the test to determine if a building is symbolic is if you can draw it in five seconds and everyone recognises it." Architect Tom Wright.

The Burj Al Arab sits just offshore in the Arabian Gulf (left and right).
Overleaf: the lower lobby and atrium, stretching 182 metres skywards.

HOW TO GET THERE
Burj Al Arab is situated just off Jumeirah Beach, 15 km south of Dubai and 25 km from Dubai International Airport, a 25-minute drive away. If you're not staying in the hotel and want to take a look around you'll need to book tea, lunch, or dinner. Dubai offers good beaches, desert safaris, fishing, golf and spas. It has a sub-tropical, arid climate, and temperatures range from 10 to 48 degrees Celsius (50 to 118 Fahrenheit).

Burj Al Arab
PO Box 74147, Dubai
United Arab Emirates
Tel: +971 4 3017777
Email: reservations@burj-al-arab.com
www.burj-al-arab.com

As the world's tallest hotel—and the only one sporting seven (albeit self-awarded) stars—Burj Al Arab boasts waterfalls, tropical reefs, an aquarium-walled restaurant, a liberal sprinkling of 24-carat gold leaf and service that would make a sultan feel molly-coddled. It sits on an artificial island in the Arabian Gulf, 280 metres from the shore, and guests are ferried from the local airport in Rolls Royces.

The image of the "Arabian Tower" is synonymous with Dubai, appearing on everything from guidebooks to car number plates. It's a well-planned strategy: Dubai ruler Sheikh Maktoum bin Rashid al-Maktoum wanted something as iconic as Sydney's Opera House or Paris' Eiffel Tower in his bid to turn the United Arab Emirates state into a world-class tourist hub. Before the oil boom of the 1960s, Dubai denizens made their living from fishing, pearling, and trading, and architect Tom Wright, of WS Atkins & Partners, drew on this seafaring past for inspiration. He delivered a design in the style of an Arabian dhow sail, and Jumeirah International opened the hotel in 1999.

To many, the Burj Al Arab represents an ostentatious level of luxury. Its 202 duplex suites each have stunning floor-to-ceiling views and personal butlers. But for the ultimate in opulence, check in to one of the royal suites on the 25th floor, which feature marble and gold staircases, private cinemas, rotating four-poster beds, and leopard-print carpets—all for around $10,000 per night. Burj Al Arab's vital statistics are equally gargantuan: its foundations sink more than 40 metres into the seabed, its diagonal trusses are as long as football pitches, and the atrium measures 182 metres high—big enough to house the Statue of Liberty.

The hotel is just one plank of the Crown Prince's tourist strategy, designed to more than double annual visitor numbers to 15 million by 2010. Most projects carry an obligatory "world's biggest and best" tag, so stand by for the world's tallest building, the globe's first luxury underwater hotel, a mammoth indoor ski resort, and 300 new islands designed in the shape of a world map.

Add this breakneck development to already booming shopping districts and you have a consumer's paradise: a thriving tourist state of giddy excess for when all that black gold finally runs dry.

Atelier sul Mare
Sicily

He tackled the Mafia, had a decade-long fight with the Sicilian authorities, and was arrested and fined—all in the name of art. It's no wonder Antonio Presti's "museum hotel" is no ordinary stay.

Antonio Presti (1957-), founder of Sicily's Atelier sul Mare.

Overleaf left to right: art rooms include Sogni tra Segni (Dreams between Signs), Il Nido (the Nest), and La Stanza del Profeta (the Room of the Prophet).

Atelier sul Mare sits innocuously at the edge of the beach at Castel di Tusa, a small fishing village on Sicily's rugged northern coast. It boasts the usual Mediterranean whitewashed walls and flower-scented terraces, but step inside and you'll find a bar covered in graffiti, a giant kiln for would-be potters, and the hotel's prime attractions—14 bizarre rooms, each designed by a leading artist. The hotel is Antonio Presti's manifesto for art—a spirited elbow in the ribs to those who dismiss modern art after just a cursory glance. The Italian believes that we should live with art. Better still, we should actually live in it, and even become part of the work itself.

Presti's love affair with art started in the 1980s, when he ploughed the family cement fortune into a series of controversial sculptures. The Fiumera d'Arte ["River of Art"] project snakes along the coast and between Sicily's Nebrodi and Madonie mountains. Despite run-ins with the Mafia, fines and court orders to remove the works, this open-air museum is still standing, and sculptors now come from all over the world to contribute.

Atelier sul Mare represents Presti's bid for a quieter life, but there are inevitably plenty of surprises. The hotel's Room of The Prophet is not for the fainthearted: turn the key and the heavy steel door crashes to the floor, guaranteeing an explosive entrance every time. The suite is an unnerving tribute to writer Pier Paolo Pasolini: a straw and mud corridor evokes the writer's favourite country of Yemen, while the bathroom's tangled weave of copper pipes are redolent of his tragic death in a car crash. Then there's Earth and Fire, with walls made entirely of shards of terracotta, or The Nest, with its giant bed eyrie. Water is a dominant theme throughout the hotel, so if you're keen on a truly relaxing stay go for the Shadow's Silhouette, with its raft bed, terrace bathtub and views of boats scudding across the Tyrrhenian Sea.

HOW TO GET THERE

The nearest airports are Palermo, 90 minutes away by car, and Catania, two hours' drive away. The hotel is well signposted on the coast road, but you'll need to turn off sharply under the railway lines towards the sea to reach the beachfront where the hotel is located. If you're travelling by train, head for Santo Stefano di Camastra, and take a local train to Castel di Tusa from there.

Atelier sul Mare
Via Cesare Battisti
4 Castel di Tusa
Messina
Sicily
Tel: +39 0921 334 295
Email: ateliersulmare@interfree.it
www.ateliersulmare.it

If you possess a burning desire to be alone and a decent pair of sunglasses, head for the world's largest salt lake in Bolivia.

"It's one of the most unreal places on earth."
Tour guide Jorge Cardenas.

Far left above and below: the entire Palacio de Sal is made of salt.
Left: the salt harvest at Salar de Uyuni, Altiplano, Bolivia.

The sheer enormity of the Salar de Uyuni in Southwest Bolivia will make your head spin. The salt lake stretches more than 10,500 square kilometres towards the Chilean border and has a solid crust measuring up to seven metres thick. And it won't be just the views that take your breath away—you'll be 3,700 metres above sea level so your lungs may struggle.

Once you've sampled the isolation of this bleached white plain, you can lay your head on a bed made, inevitably, out of the area's most plentiful material. The rustic Salt Palace Hotel, or Palacio de Sal, sits on the edge of the salt flats and is every inch a slug's worst nightmare. The walls, tables, chairs and beds are entirely made of sodium chloride, harvested from the flats outside. The only salt-free zones are mattresses and toilets, making a night's stay far more comfortable than it sounds.

Palacio de Sal is the brainchild of Juan Quesada, an entrepreneurial tour operator who was convinced that a quirky night's stay would appeal to the thousands of tourists who visit the flats every year. He worked with native Aymara Teodoro Colque to build a small salt hotel in 1994, opening the grander Palacio de Sal in 1996. Quesada continues to run the hotel, which now boasts 34 rooms, a salt-water spa, and even an 18-hole golf course.

Your visit will be a memorable stop-off on an incredible tour of the Bolivian *altiplano*. Trips take in shimmering green lakes, dusty cowboy terrain, giant cacti, Andean mountain ranges, extinct volcanoes, geysers and hot springs. And after all that visual stimulation, who wouldn't want a few hours of uncluttered white space?

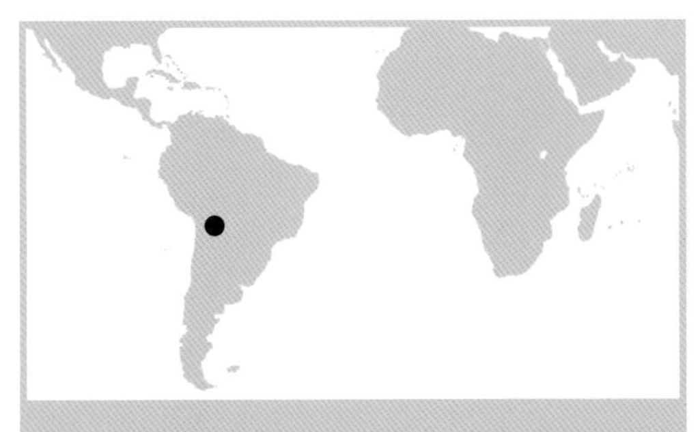

HOW TO GET THERE

A popular route is to fly to La Paz, pick up a bus to Oruro and a train from there to Uyuni, where you'll find numerous tours of the area's highlights. Be prepared for plummeting temperatures—it can drop to minus 10 degrees Celsius (14 degrees Fahrenheit) at night. A smattering of Spanish really helps as English is not widely spoken outside Bolivia's main cities.

Hotel Palacio de Sal
Uyuni Saltflats
Near Colchani
Bolivia
Tel: + 5912 622 5186
Email: uyusalht@entelnet.bo
www.magri-amexpress.com.bo
www.salardeuyuni.net

Lake Palace Hotel
India

James Bond fantasists be warned: a trip to Udaipur's Lake Palace Hotel will see you ordering vodka martinis in a ridiculous Scottish accent and tussling with phantom megalomaniacs at every turn.

"Nothing but marble enters into their composition, columns, baths, reservoirs, fountains, all are of this material, often inlaid with mosaics, and the uniformity pleasingly diversified by the light passing through glass of every hue."
Colonel James Tod.

The Lake Palace sits in the centre of Lake Pichola (left) and features gardens and several stunning suites (far left).

That 007 feeling is justified: this "floating" hotel was the baddies' lair in the 1983 film *Octopussy*, and the chances are you'll be touring the town's forts and palaces in a white Ambassador car with a private driver.

The hotel doesn't actually float. It's reassuringly anchored to an island of solid granite. Just getting there is a truly exotic experience, particularly if you travel after dusk. Wait for a few minutes at the lake's edge and a launch will carry you gently across to candle-lit steps and a Raj-style welcome from immaculately dressed staff.

The Lake Palace Hotel is one of the finest examples of Mogul–Rajput architecture, characterised by domes and finely sculpted pillars and arches. Inside there is a tranquil courtyard of filigree screens, ponds and fountains, a swimming pool and lily pond, restaurants with stunning views of the lake and town, and opulent suites adorned with stained-glass windows and Rajasthani art. Sounds fit for a king? That's exactly what it's meant to be. The hotel was originally built as a summer palace for Maharana Jagat Singh II, a profligate Mewar ruler with a penchant for the arts but a weak handle on local politics.

Founded in the 6th century AD, the Mewar dynasty managed to fend off all manner of attacks from rival factions for more than a millennium, but in the 18th century the family faced extinction at the hands of the Marathas, mercenary chieftains from the south. The Marathas took Udaipur in 1736, and Maharana Jagat Singh II responded with characteristic obliviousness, kick-starting an extravagant building programme which saw the Lake Palace inaugurated in 1746. His inadequate leadership plunged the dynasty into a long-running round of civil war, financial disaster, and tussles over the crown.

Despite the ineffectiveness of Jagat Singh II the Mewars managed to survive, and are now the world's longest-serving dynasty. Ironically the palace itself is now helping to secure the family's future: Maharana Bhagwat Singh converted the place into a hotel in 1961, wisely cashing in on India's tourist boom.

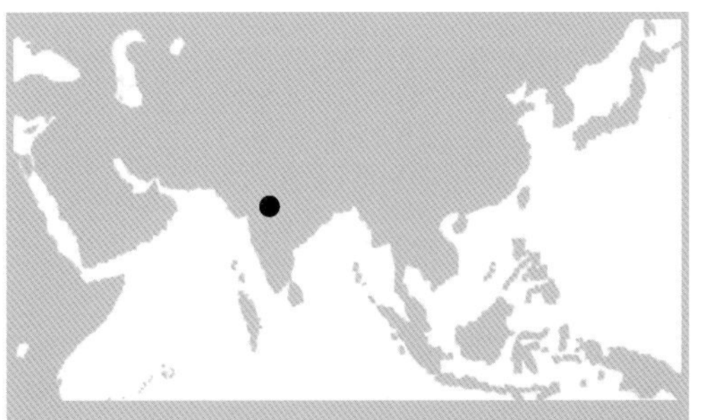

HOW TO GET THERE

The nearest airport is 24 km from Udaipur, and there are daily flights to Delhi and Mumbai and many other cities across India. A much more sociable way to travel is by train, although remember you'll have to book a day or two in advance. Once in Udaipur you'll find plenty of autorickshaws and taxis to take you to Lake Pichola. If you're not staying at the Lake Palace Hotel you'll have to book a meal to take a look inside. Udaipur is one of the country's most tourist-friendly towns and a good base for exploring Rajasthan.

Taj Lake Palace
Post Box No.5
Lake Pichola
Udaipur 313 001
Rajasthan
India
Tel: + 91 294 2528800
Email: lakepalace.udaipur@tajhotels.com
www.tajhotels.com

"The most diversified and most romantic spot on the continent of India." Colonel James Tod on Udaipur.
Below: a launch takes guests across the lake.

Hotel im Wasserturm
Germany

As a barometer of Anglo-German relations, you can't get much more spectacular than Europe's largest water tower.

"One of those rare places where beauty, comfort and well-being come together in perfect harmony."
Film director Claude Chabrol.

Right and overleaf: the water tower's original wrought iron staircase was restored as part of the conversion. The hotel also boasts an 11-metre-high atrium.

This tower was designed by English architect John Moorlands in the 19th century, but the Allies managed to blitz more than eight metres off the monolith in World War II. Now converted into a luxury hotel, it's a favourite bolthole of an international crowd including well-heeled Brits, film directors, royal personages, and assorted Hollywood stars.

The water tower was built in 1868 but was defunct by the turn of the century thanks to a new underground water system, which was introduced to cope with Cologne's booming population. The 35.5-metre-tall brick cylinder was then used as a workshop, storehouse, and air-raid shelter before investors bought it in 1984.

Architect Konrad L. Heinrich had his work cut out to create the hotel's 11 storeys, particularly as the tower was a listed monument. The $75 million conversion included removing 20,000 tonnes of rubble, a 300,000-brick rebuild, and the mammoth task of restoring the original cast-iron staircase that corkscrews through building. The reception hall alone is a major feat, more than 11 metres high with connecting walkways.

Of course, a world-leading hotel needs a world-leading interior designer and Andrée Putman gladly obliged. The *Parisienne*, who designed Concorde's interior, was a major force in the invention of the boutique hotel, having designed Paris's Pershing Hall and the Morgans hotel in New York. For the Hotel im Wasserturm Putman created an Art Deco-influenced minimalist interior inspired by the tower's curves, using liberal splashes of aqua blue and brick to reflect its origins. When you visit, make sure you check out the Michelin-starred rooftop restaurant: it's a good place to pick out the city's highlights and plan your itinerary.

Cologne is Germany's oldest city, a friendly, cosmopolitan place with a vibrant arts scene. And once you've had your fill of the Gothic cathedral, museums and galleries, cobbled streets, parks and street entertainers, seek out Cologne's two famous restoratives—Kölsch beer and chocolate.

HOW TO GET THERE

The nearest airports are Cologne-Bonn (14 km) and Düsseldorf International (60 km): you'll find frequent trains to the city centre from each. Hotel im Wasserturm is 1 km from the centre of Cologne, and 200 m from the Poststrasse underground stop.

Hotel im Wasserturm
Kaygasse 2
50676 Cologne
Germany
Tel: +49 (0) 221 200 80
Email: info@hotel-im-wasserturm.de
www.hotel-im-wasserturm.de

Ice Hotel
Sweden

The heat of a sauna led to an ice-cold idea in Swedish Lapland, 200 kilometres inside the Arctic Circle.

"It's like a dream. People who are come find it fascinating, and I stay in the hotel five or six times a year."
Yngve Bergqvist, founder of the Ice Hotel.

Far left: the Ice Hotel's chilly confines.
Left: the hotel's replica Globe Theatre.

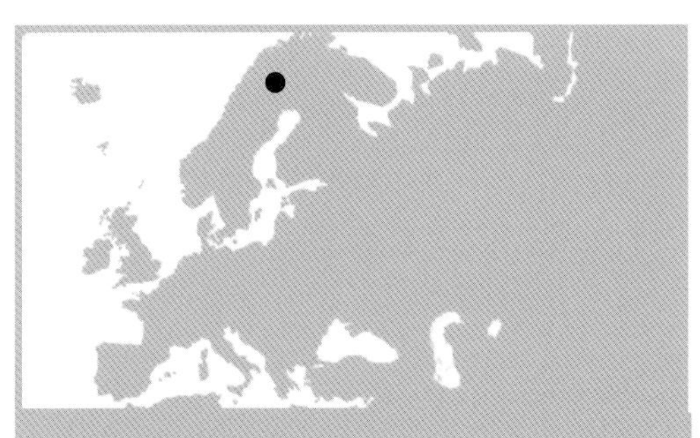

It appears to be the most hare-brained scheme in the world. The entire hotel, including sweeping entrance, pillars, walls, furniture, and sculpture, is made of ice. Every winter workers build a new hotel using 30,000 tonnes of snow and 4,000 tonnes of ice harvested from the Torneälven River. And every spring, the whole place melts and runs back into the river under the midnight sun. Inside it's a chilly minus five degrees Celsius (23 degrees Fahrenheit), and guests are zipped into survival bags to sleep on ice-block beds padded with reindeer skins.

The hotel's origins date back to the late 1980s. Yngve Bergqvist was taking a sauna in the Swedish village of Jukkasjärvi, and was discussing with friends how he could attract visitors to his holiday cottages during the quiet winter months. The steam-powered brainstorm hit upon the idea of a winter hotel, and Bergqvist promptly set off on a fact-finding tour of the world's chilliest climes—taking in Sapporo's ice festival in Japan, Alaska and Minnesota in the US, and the furthest reaches of Lapland.

"When I came back I was thinking maybe we could use ice and snow to build a house," said Bergqvist. He spent four years experimenting with designs, but it wasn't until 1990 that his igloo had its first real test: "Some friends wanted to stay," explained Bergqvist, "but it was the only night of the winter that our hotel was booked up, so I said they could stay in the our new ice hotel." The guests found the sub-zero overnighter thoroughly exhilarating. "We had a party half the night and they still talk about it to this day," added Bergqvist. The Ice Hotel was born.

This bizarre formula became a massive success. The hotel has grown to more than 80 times its original size, each year boasting a new design. Between December and May thousands of visitors come to sample its vodka bar, cinema, and Shakespeare-style Globe Theatre. There's even a chapel and bridal suite, making it a hit with couples with a penchant for fur wedding attire. Outside the hotel's icy confines you can jump on a snow sledge, snowmobile, or skis to explore the wilderness and sample indigenous Sámi culture with a meal around a campfire and a spot of reindeer herding. It's also a great place to see the inspiring swathes of green, purple, blue and yellow lights of the Aurora Borealis. And if the cold really gets to you, there's always a very good sauna that Yngve Bergqvist can recommend.

HOW TO GET THERE

The Ice Hotel is located 12 km from Kiruna airport and 17 km from Kiruna train station. There are buses from Kiruna bus station from Monday to Friday, and the hotel will arrange transfers from Kiruna airport or train station. Most guests spend just one night in the main hotel before decamping to one of the modern, heated cabins next door. Also, make sure to reserve well in advance—the Ice Hotel gets very booked up, particularly at weekends.

Ice Hotel AB
981 91 Jukkasjärvi
Sweden
Tel: +46 980 66 800 or toll-free number within Sweden: 020 29 14 33
Email: info@icehotel.com
www.icehotel.com

Reindeer skins cushion the ice beds and sculptures are always a big feature of the hotel.
Bottom left: a performance of Hamlet at the hotel's replica Globe Theatre.
Bottom right: Albert Falck's Noah's Ark suite.

Can an airport or a suitcase really provide inspiration for a house? This avant-garde, and thoroughly capitalist, enclave near the Great Wall of China proves anything is possible.

Left: Shigeru Ban's Furniture House, where the furniture is the primary influence in the design. Right: a view from the Clubhouse across to the Great Wall.

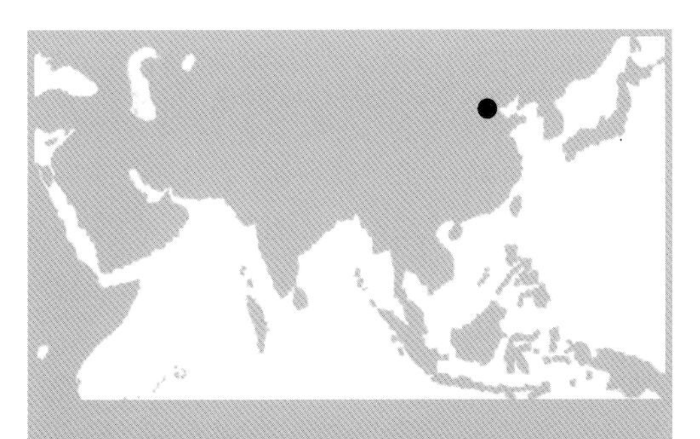

HOW TO GET THERE
The nearest airport is Beijing Capital Airport, 60 km away. The Commune is around 60 km (1 hour) from downtown Bejing. By car, head out of the city on the Badaling Expressway and exit at Shuiguan Great Wall. The commune is clearly signposted from there. You can hire a car and driver from Bejing. If you can't afford the villa's prices, you can pay around $14.50 for a low-budget look around.

Commune by the Great Wall
The Great Wall Shuiguan exit
Badaling Expressway
Beijing 102102
China
Tel: +86 10 6567 3333 (ext 323, 328)
or +86 10 8118 1888
Email: reservation@commune.com.cn
www.commune.com.cn

When it comes to attracting jet-setters with extremely deep pockets the Commune by the Great Wall probably leads the field. This architectural showcase is a boutique hotel featuring 11 cutting-edge villas and a clubhouse, each designed by a high-profile Asian architect. Feted by both the architectural and travel press, the villas are also popular venues for corporate junkets, hosting press launches and parties, fashion shows, and high-powered meetings.

There's a fitting "rags-to-riches" story attached. The commune was founded by property developers Pan Shiyi and Zhang Xin—now a high profile "It" couple and willing role models for China's burgeoning middle class. Pan Shiyi grew up in a small village, and hard times meant that two of his sisters were brought up by another family. He set up a property company in Bejing in 1992, cashing in on the soaring price of office space. Meanwhile, Zhang Xin worked alongside her mother in the sweatshops of Hong Kong before studying economics in England and going on to work for Goldman Sachs.

The couple set up their property company, SOHO China, in 1995, selling "small office, home office" units inspired by New York's famous arty district. Their original plan was to build the commune as a series of private houses, but they decided to follow the boutique hotel route after the development bagged a special architectural prize at the 2002 Venice Biennale.

When you visit be sure to see the commune's most popular villa—the six-bedroomed Bamboo Wall. Designed by Japanese architect Kengo Kuma, the serene space boasts great views of the historic wall and a showpiece Zen-style tearoom complete with pool. You should also take a look at Gary Chang's Suitcase, a Rietveld-style configurable house with mobile floors and screens allowing you to modify room sizes at will.

China may be embracing Western consumerism with abandon, but it's good to see someone pushing architectural boundaries as well as capitalist values.

"We had a vision in mind when we built the Commune. As developers we are aware that what we build today will set the landscape of Chinese architecture for the next 100 years. Our vision is to influence a whole generation of architects, developers, consumers in China."
Zhang Xin of developers SOHO China

Far left: Kengo Kuma's serene Bamboo Wall.
Left: interior and exterior of Kanika R'Kul's Shared House.

Below: Seung H-Sang's Clubhouse sits at the centre of the development, housing communal facilities such as bars and a restaurant. Right: the Suitcase House, designed by Gary Chang where living quarters can be tidily concealed beneath floor panels to create a clutter-free space.

Rogner-Bad Blumau Hotel & Spa
Austria

He made rousing speeches in the nude and changed his name to "realm of peace one hundred waters." To many, Friedensreich Hundertwasser wasn't exactly the obvious choice to design an Austrian spa hotel.

"The straight line is something cowardly drawn with a rule, without thought or feeling; it is a line which does not exist in nature." Hundertwasser's poem, *The Paradise Destroyed by the Straight Line*.

Friedensreich Hundertwasser (1928–2000) was born Friedrich Stowasser but changed his name in 1949.

Left: the hotel sprouts trees from its roof and sports a huge onion dome (overleaf)—typically witty Hundertwasser touches.

HOW TO GET THERE
The nearest airports are Graz (60 km; 40 minutes' drive) and Vienna (130 km; 90 minutes). Alternatively you can catch the train to Bad Blumau station and someone from the hotel will pick you up. You have a choice of double rooms, apartments, and suites. If you tire of the spas, then horse riding, cycling, tennis, and golf provide stimulating alternatives.

Rogner-Bad Blumau Hotel & Spa
A-8283 Bad Blumau 100
Tel: +43 (0)3383 5100-0
Email: spa.blumau@rogner.com
www.blumau.com

Hundertwasser was hardly an ordinary architect. His formal training spanned just three months and he loved picking fights with the architectural establishment. This commission, however, proved to be worth the risk. Rogner-Bad Blumau is Hundertwasser at his best: a fairytale hotchpotch of natural contours, multi-coloured façades and onion-domed towers.

You'll find the spa hotel arching among the hills of Styria in eastern Austria. Roofs are grassed and sprout shrubs and trees, while the hotel's centrepiece is a magical thermal pool. And you can't fail to leave the place feeling about 20 years younger: it boasts hot springs, a cool pool, Roman and Turkish baths, and a welter of spa treatments and holistic therapies.

The design is part ode to the beauty of nature, part witty tirade against the straight line. Hundertwasser hated geometrical rigour, insisting that straight lines created speed and stress. Originally a painter, he was a major fan of the Secessionist movement (the Viennese version of Art Nouveau) and went on to design schools, stamps, flags, museums, and churches in his trademark bold, almost naïve, style. His equally surreal Hundertwasser Haus, a technicoloured apartment block with trees growing out of the rooms, is one of Vienna's biggest tourist attractions.

You can see the influence of Hundertwasser's eclectic experiences throughout this hotel. Its decorative elements were inspired by his extensive travels throughout North Africa, France, Italy, Japan and Uganda, and he was also heavily influenced by fellow Austrian artists Gustav Klimt and Egon Schiele.

The spa hotel continues to be grist to the mill of Hundertwasser's detractors, who accuse him of creating people-pleasing, fantasy-riddled kitsch. His response, undoubtedly, would be an echo of his 1958 manifesto against rationalism in architecture: "The time has come for people to rebel against their confinement in cubical constructions like chickens or rabbits in cages, a confinement which is alien to human nature." When rebellion is this relaxing, who could disagree?

Acknowledgements

Writing this book has been an adventure in itself. I'd like to thank my publisher, Philippa Hurd, for charting its path, avoiding nasty cliff edges and packing the emergency croissants. I'm indebted to her for such persistence and dedication in the face of several force-nine challenges. My heartfelt thanks also go to Stu Smith and his design team for conjuring up such a cracking layout. Kieran Wyatt and Caroline Jones have made an indefatigable proofing and fact-checking duo; I'm grateful to them both for their enthusiasm and general ribaldry. Thanks also to Paul Vater, who provided the introduction that turned a scribble on a piece of paper into something pretty impressive. My biggest thanks are reserved for my wife, Sarah, who has spent many months keeping my spirits up and my stress levels down. Thank you.

A worldwide network of kind individuals has helped me write these chapters, so I raise a figurative glass of beer/sangria/vodka/sake/green tea in recognition of their input and support.

Thanks to:
Augusto Areal, Sylvie Béguelin, Sabine Bergmann, Miguel Angel Bolaños, Marta Batko, Yngve Bergqvist, Lucy Blogg, Christophe Bonin, Sofia Brignone, Dan Buck, Katherine Byrne, Stefania Canta, Jorge Cardenas, Tom Chudleigh, Kylie Clark, Jean-Baptiste Clerc, Norbert Cymbalista, Amanda Dahlquist, Antonella Deiana, Lucy Ellison, Susana Erdozain, Patrick Filmer-Sankey, Keith Garner, Marcelo Gavirati, Constanze Grininger, Jackie Gully, Sigal Hachili, Joram Harel, Tim Heffley, Jose Herrasti, Pål Hivand, Victoria Hubbard, Phil Jackson, Mark Jones, Graeme Kelleher, Bernard Khoury, Nicola King, Stuart Klawans, Christina Sophia Lambertz, Derek Latham, Julian Lee, Karine Letayf, Joanne Looby, Jonathan McKeever, Eric McNevin, John Maizels, Liz Middleton, Gianfranco Molino, Adriana Navarro, Alan Perry, John Pilkington, Jean Pipete, Charles Provine, David Rowe, Ian Rumgay, Javier Senosiain, Yuko Shimizu, Helena Sjöholm, Isabel Sole, Tim Smit, Maurice Snowden, Margo Stipe, Nina Telebak, Jenny Thompson, Catherine Visser, Flo Wallace, Raiqah Ripa Walie, Chunlei Wang, Barbara Weil, Ann Welch, Vivi Wickström, Charlotte Wilmots, Amanda Wilson, Victoria Winkelman, Tom Wright, Rupert Youngman, Elena Zanini, Boris Zeisser.

Many thanks to the following organisations for providing information for this book:
24H architecture, ADCK-Centre Culturel Tjibaou, Arcosanti, Atelier sul Mare, Battersea Power Station Community Group, Bernard Khoury Architects, Bodegas Ysios, British Council, Bangladesh, CC Africa Tanzania, Eric Owen Moss Architects, *Financial Times*, Frank Lloyd Wright Archives, Fundación César Manrique, Future Systems, Glaskogens Naturreservat, Government of Dubai, Department of Tourism and Commerce Marketing, Graz Tourismus, Guinness Storehouse, Hotel im Wasserturm, Hotel Villa de Laguardia, Il Vittoriale degli Italiani, Japan National Tourist Organization, Jersey Tourism, Kengo Kuma & Associates, Kopalnia Soli "Wieliczka" Trasa Turystyczna sp. z o.o., Kunsthaus Graz, LA Tourism.Com, Le Palais Idéal du Facteur Cheval, Longleat, Mango PR, Meadows School of the Arts, Southern Methodist University, Nek Chand Foundation and *Raw Vision* magazine, Parkview International London Plc, Reef HQ Aquarium, Renzo Piano Building Workshop s.r.l., ScottishArchitecture.com, SOHO China Ltd., Solomon R. Guggenheim Foundation, St Lawrence and St Matthew's Church, Jersey, Studio Daniel Libeskind, Tel Aviv University, The Dovetail Agency, The Eden Project, The Kreisberg Group, The Minack Theatre, WS Atkins & Partners.

Publisher's Acknowledgements

The Publisher is grateful to the following for their help in the preparation of this book:

Sofia Brignone; Hugh Clarke; Doug Creedon, Jersey Tourist Office; Julia Elmore and John Maizels, *Raw Vision*; Mauro Guglielminotti; Natalie Hill, National Monuments Record; Martin Krautter, Erco; Tecla, Museo-Albergo, Atelier sul Mare; Geraint Jennings, La Société Jersiaise; Christina Sophia Lambertz, Hotel im Wasserturm; Paul Stephens; Misty Stinson, MILD Graphics; John Warburton-Lee; Chris Waterman, WS Atkins & Partners.

Credits

Le Palais Idéal du Facteur Cheval: Ferdinand Cheval's letter to the Hauterives department archivist André Lacroix (thought to date from 1897).
"The Postman's Palace" by Jeremy Josephs at www.jeremyjosephs.com.
Centre Culturel Tjibaou - ADCK/Renzo Piano Building Workshop, Architectes.
"Survey - Singapore - Cosmopolitan city for work and play." Business Guide by Douglas Wong in *Financial Times*, April 12, 2002.
The Royal Pavilion, Libraries & Museums, Brighton & Hove.
Hundertwasser Archive.
The Nek Chand Foundation and *Raw Vision* magazine.
Commission for the Commemoration of the 150th Anniversary of the Birth of Antoni Gaudí.
The Building by Matthew Drutt at www.guggenheim.org.
Fondazione Il Vittoriale degli Italiani
Interview with Peter Cook by Caroline Ednie, June 18, 2004 at ScottishArchitecture.com.
Kisho Kurokawa, *Philosophy of Symbiosis*, (London: Academy Editions, 1994).
Louis Kahn, *Perspecta* 4, 2 (1957).
Colonel James Tod, Annals and Antiquities of Rajasthan (1829).
The Friends of Carhenge.
The *Cornishman* newspaper.
Le Corbusier, *Towards a New Architecture*, (New York: Payson and Clarke, 1927).

p. 29 left: © Bill Heinsohn / Alamy
pp. 30–31 Courtesy of Kisho Kurokawa
pp. 32–35 Photos: Sofia Brignone
p. 36 top: John Pilkington
bottom: Jonathan Lee
p. 37 right: Jonathan Lee
left: © Bettmann/Corbis
pp. 38–39 Panorama Stock Photos Co Ltd / Alamy
p. 40 david sanger photography / Alamy
p. 41 top: Jon Bower / Alamy
bottom left: Felix Stensson / Alamy
bottom right: Panorama Stock Photos Co Ltd / Alamy
p. 42 Tom Chudleigh
p. 43 left: Troy and Mary Parlee / Alamy
right: Tom Chudleigh
p. 44 Mauro Guglielminotti
p. 45 left: Mauro Guglielminotti
right: POPPERFOTO / Alamy
pp. 46–47 Mauro Guglielminotti
pp. 48–51 © Mitsumasa Fujitsuka, courtesy of Kengo Kuma & Associates
p. 52 PhotoBliss / Alamy
p. 53 right: Michelle Chaplow / Alamy
p. 54 left: Tin Roof Images / Alamy
right: eye35.com / Alamy
p. 55 scenicireland.com / Christopher Hill Photographic / Alamy
p. 56 LifeFile Photos Ltd / Alamy
p. 57 left: LifeFile Photos Ltd / Alamy
pp. 58–59 Worldwide Picture Library / Alamy
p. 60 © Richard Davies
pp. 61–63 Courtesy of Future Systems
p. 64 top: David B. Brownlee
bottom: © 2002–2005 Estate of Roberto Schezen
p. 65 left: Jiri Rezac / Alamy
p. 66 © 2002–2005 Estate of Roberto Schezen
p. 67 Kazi Khaleed Ashraf
p. 68 bitterbredt.de
p. 69 Barbara Weil
pp. 70–73 bitterbredt.de
pp. 74–75 © Erco Leuchten GmbH
pp. 76–79 Courtesy of Eric Owen Moss
p. 80 Robert Harding Picture Library Ltd / Alamy
p. 81 left and centre: Reproduced by permission of English Heritage.NMR
p. 81 right: RIBA Library Photographs Collection
pp. 82–83 Courtesy of The Guinness Storehouse Museum
pp. 84 © John Warburton-Lee/John Warburton-Lee Photography
p. 85 left: © John Warburton-Lee/John Warburton-Lee Photography
right: Photo: Suzanne DeChillo/The New York Times
pp. 86–87 © John Warburton-Lee/John Warburton-Lee Photography
pp. 88–89 MILD Graphics
pp. 90–93 © Pino Musi, courtesy of Studio Botta
pp. 94–97 Courtesy of Le Palais Idéal du Facteur Cheval
p. 98 © Hugh Clarke
p. 99 left: © Hugh Clarke
right: Boots Photographic Archive, Nottingham
p. 100 Achim Bednorz/© VG Bild-Kunst, Bonn 2005
p. 101 left: Bildarchiv Monheim GmbH / Alamy
p. 102 Bildarchiv Monheim GmbH / Alamy
p. 103 wim wiskerke / Alamy
p. 104 Network Photographers / Alamy
p. 105 Robert Harding Picture Library Ltd / Alamy
p. 106 top left and right: Devinder Sangha / Alamy
bottom: Network Photographers / Alamy
p. 107: Devinder Sangha / Alamy
pp. 108–113 Courtesy of Wieliczka Salt Mine
pp. 114–117 Photos by Eujin Goh and Jonathan Rose; courtesy of Wilford Schupp Architekten GmbH
pp. 118–121 David Rowe, courtesy of The Eden Project
pp. 122–123 Courtesy of Bernard Khoury
p. 124 top and bottom: ARTUR/Monika Nikolic
p. 125 left: RIBA Library Photographs Collection
right: ARTUR/Paul Rafferty/VIEW
pp. 126–28 allOver photography / Alamy
p. 129 top: Pat Behnke / Alamy
bottom: David Stares / Alamy
p. 130 Longleat House, Wiltshire
p. 131 left: © Skyscan Photolibrary
right: © David Partner
p. 132 © Michael Freeman, London
p. 133 left: RIBA Library Photographs Collection
right: David Heald © The Solomon R. Guggenheim Foundation, New York
pp. 134–35 © Michael Freeman, London
pp. 136 top: Photo: Maggie Jones Maizels, courtesy of *Raw Vision*
bottom left and right: Jonathan Lee
pp. 137–39 Photos: Maggie Jones Maizels, courtesy of *Raw Vision*
p. 140 © SAPPORO DOME
p. 141 right: © SAPPORO DOME
p. 142 Photo: Michel Denancé © RPBW, Renzo Piano Building Workshop
p. 143 left: Photo: John Gollings © RPBW, Renzo Piano Building Workshop
p. 143 right: RIBA Library Photographs Collection
pp. 144–45 Photo: John Gollings © RPBW, Renzo Piano Building Workshop
pp. 146–47 Courtesy of Reef HQ
pp. 148–151 © Paul Stephens 2002–2005
p. 152 © John Warburton-Lee/John Warburton-Lee Photography
p. 153 Images of Africa Photobank / Alamy
pp. 154–55 © John Warburton-Lee/John Warburton-Lee Photography
pp. 156–57 Courtesy of The Landmark Trust
pp. 158–61 © Jumeirah International
p. 162 top and bottom: Pippa Hurd
p. 163 left: Pippa Hurd
right: Archivio Fiumara d'Arte
pp. 164–65 Archivio Fiumara d'Arte
p. 166 top: Jamie Marshall / Alamy
bottom: Gary Cook / Alamy
p. 167 © Gary Cook / Alamy
p. 168 top: Stuart Abraham / Alamy
bottom: AM Corporation / Alamy
p. 169 IFA Munich, Aberham
p. 170 © John Warburton-Lee/John Warburton-Lee Photography
p. 171 © John Warburton-Lee/John Warburton-Lee Photography
pp. 172–75 Courtesy of Hotel im Wasserturm
pp. 176–77 Robin Whalley / Alamy
p. 178 top: Robin Whalley / Alamy
bottom: Nick Hanna / Alamy
p. 179 top: Robin Whalley / Alamy
bottom: Nick Hanna / Alamy
p. 180 top and bottom: Satoshi Asakawa
p. 181 Ma Xiaochun
pp. 182–185 Satoshi Asakawa
p. 186 Copyright © Hundertwasser Architekturprojekt
pp. 187–89 Bildagentur Franz Waldhaeusl / Alamy

Index of Names
Numbers in *italics* refer to captions